creative ESSENTIALS

Craig Batty

SCREENPLAYS

how to write and sell them

creative ESSENTIALS

First published in 2012 by Kamera Books
an imprint of Oldcastle Books,
PO Box 394, Harpenden, Herts, AL5 1XJ
www.kamerabooks.com

Copyright © Craig Batty 2012
Series Editor: Hannah Patterson

A CIP catalogue record for this book is available from the British Library.

978-1-84243-503-8 (Print)
978-1-84243-643-1 (epub)
978-1-84243-642-4 (kindle)
978-1-84243-644-8 (pdf)

2 4 6 8 10 9 7 5 3 1

Typeset by Elsa Mathern in Franklin Gothic 9 pt
Printed and Bound by CPI Group (UK) ltd, Croydon, CR0 4YY

ACKNOWLEDGEMENTS

To family, friends and students who've played their part in the making of this book. In particular, to RMIT students in the Anatomy of a Screenplay class, who were both insightful and inspiring. To Hannah for commissioning the book, and to Anne for doing a brilliant job editing it. To all the great screenwriters and filmmakers out there who've given me wonderful material to write about. And to all the book's readers – may it serve you well.

CONTENTS

INTRODUCTION

Oh no, not another screenwriting book! And that's just what *I* thought.

But then, when I thought about it some more, I realised we *do* need good screenwriting books; that, in fact, there's quite a shortage of them. While there may be hundreds on the market, few of them actually speak to the writer, telling them instead what they should and shouldn't be doing. What's missing is a sense of conversation, a sense that the author knows what the writer's trying to do, and so speaks to them in a way that's helpful and personal, as well as insightful.

I want this book to speak to you as a writer, to connect with what you're going through – good or bad – as you develop your screenplay, and to inspire you to move forward, helping you to find solutions that you're happy with and that you believe in. Above all, I want this book to be a guide that you come back to again and again, if not for help with a specific screenplay problem, then as a guilty pleasure – perhaps reminding you that, yes, you do know what you're doing. And I use the word *guide* intentionally here. It's not a rule book. Nor is it a set of principles, techniques, tricks, tips, etc.

Over the last nine years, I've worked with lots of screenwriters, student screenwriters, professional screenwriters, emerging screen-writers, and people who write screenplays as a hobby. I've read lots of screenplays and screen ideas (treatments, outlines) – at least a thousand – and I've discovered that I love working with screenwriters on their screenplays. Writing your own material is one thing – and I love that, too – but to work closely with someone on their idea is something else. There's a buzz that comes from talking about characters, plots, themes, visual images and dialogue – it's like chatting to your friends about a film when you come out of the cinema, only better. There's even more of a frisson when you can see the passion rising in a writer; when you can see them getting excited about their screenplay, and talking about it with much more verve. And here's the thing: the best buzz of all comes from seeing a writer suddenly make the leap into finding their own solutions. They've 'got' what they've been trying to achieve, and suddenly they fly. As a guide, a mentor, you get real satisfaction from this moment.

I've also written a lot about screenwriting. Some of you might be familiar with my first book, *Writing for the Screen: Creative and Critical Approaches* (2008), which was written with Zara Waldebäck. The response to that has been really positive. Not because we're saying things that are explicitly new, but because we wrote it in a way that was intended to be helpful and inspiring. We touched on the idea of creativity, too, and how often in screenwriting training there's a lack of attention paid to the creative process – it's all about craft, technique and industry. Although these things are very important, they're nothing without creativity. A screenwriter is a creative writer, after all. So we decided to follow this up with a second book, *The Creative Screenwriter: Exercises to Expand Your Craft* (2012). Quite different in tone and format, this book offers a plethora of creative writing exercises intended to deepen the screenwriter's understanding of key aspects of screenwriting – character, structure, theme, dialogue, pitching, developing ideas, etc. I also wrote the book *Movies That Move Us: Screenwriting and the Power of the Protagonist's Journey* (2011), which, in essence, develops Christopher Vogler's famous Hero's Journey model to take into account both the physical and the emotional journey experienced by a protagonist. There's quite a lot of theory in that book, but there are six case studies of famous films that highlight the points I'm making. Vogler himself endorsed the book, which was very nice. I don't expect everyone to agree with my ideas

– how boring life would be if they did – and I know that there will be things I've missed or seen differently to others. But I'm certain there will be something in this book that will connect with you; something that will make you see and understand screenwriting in a different way than before. I'll not see the recognition in your eyes – the passion rising – but I'll know it's there.

So, I hope you find this book useful, and I hope you enjoy it. In the end, we write because we get pleasure from it. There are times when we utterly despise our art – we can't get the plot right, the character doesn't sound right and nobody likes the screenplay – but we only despise it because we love it so much. And, because we get so much joy out of it, we want it to be perfect, and we want others to enjoy it, too. Rather than seeing this book as a chore, then – something you've got to read for university, or plough through to see where you might be going wrong – try to relish working through the material. Let it guide your own thoughts and feelings about good screenwriting. Have fun thinking of your own examples. And, where it feels appropriate, enjoy having your own alternative readings, or the fact that you disagree with what I've said!

1. THE NATURE OF SCREENWRITING

A few years ago, when I was delivering a workshop on creativity at the London Screenwriters' Festival, three men walked out. As they left, one of them mumbled something along the lines of, 'This is ridiculous… creativity's got nothing to do with screenwriting.' Maybe it was the way I was pitching it – though I'd only been talking for about five minutes – but creativity and screenwriting not connecting? Being creative having nothing to do with screenwriting? Well, actually, this is a view that many people have. But it's wrong. Screenwriting is creative writing. It's perhaps got more of a business slant to it than other kinds of fiction, but it's still creative writing. And it's through developing creativity that a screenwriter can make a film leap from being formulaic to formidable.

For those who stayed in the workshop – about 40 of them – we proved that, by thinking 'outside the box', ideas were strengthened and stories became more engaging and original. Some of the writers realised that their ideas had to be abandoned in favour of new ones that emerged – but that's what it's all about. After all, who wants to stick with an idea just for the sake of it, when there's a better one out there waiting to be tackled?

Nevertheless, a common perception is that screenwriting is driven by business. In one way, it is – there's a lot of money involved usually, and many more people needed to make a film possible, which of course brings with it financial risks. The development of a screenplay also leans more towards the business-driven model, with more people vying for their voice to be heard, and more 'at stake' when people like the director and financier get involved. All of this is important, and screenwriters should know about these kinds of factors, but that doesn't mean that creativity should be sidelined. Being a screenwriter is still about being creative. It's about having the ability to see things in different and interesting ways and, when the going gets tough, being able to find creative solutions to problems – your problems or other people's problems (which you might very well have to take on board).

> **Creative exercise**
> How are you creative? What does creativity mean to you? Thinking specifically about your life as a screenwriter – however long it may be, or experienced you are – make a list of all the things you do that you'd categorise as creative. These might be decisions you make, or actions you take. When you've done this, make a list of all the things you do that you'd categorise as business oriented. How does the list look? Are there clear connections between creative and business decisions and actions – and if not, how might you try and connect them?

JUST A WORKING DOCUMENT?

Another common perception is that the screenplay is only a working document. It's an artefact that will be turned into something else entirely – the film. So it goes from being a static, paper-based thing to a live piece of moving image. Although this is technically correct, it's philosophically incorrect. A screenplay isn't static at all – aside from the fact that it'll go through many re-writes, it's a document full of life. You don't just read a screenplay because you want to understand how the film will be made – you read it because it's a good story in itself, one that has the power to entertain and move you. The action on the page runs through your mind as you read. The dialogue comes to life in your head. Even the pace of the story emerges through the way the screenplay's been written – the overall structure and scene-by-scene construction. Because a screenplay is written in the active voice, in present tense, it speaks to you as you read it. Your imagination works just as much as it might when reading a novel. So a screenplay isn't 'just' a working document. It's a well-crafted and experiential piece of writing, one that will hopefully be made into a film afterwards.

More will be said later about writing the actual text of a screenplay, but, for now, think about all the ways in which you might create a 'good read' on the page. Think about how you might use evocative language to capture the reader's attention. About how you might use the layout of the page to help give a sense of the feel of a scene. About how you might connect scenes to punctuate meaning and build pace. And about how dialogue might be carefully crafted to complement or juxtapose with what we're seeing on the screen.

Creative exercise

Get hold of a screenplay – hopefully you're reading them regularly! – and think specifically about how the writing on the page is connecting you with the story (or not). What does the page look like? What kinds of description are being used – if any – in the screen directions? Which feelings are being evoked by what's on the page, and how's that being done? How do you know whether you should be empathising with a character or not? What's the screenwriter giving you?

LAYOUT

There's no point in giving a really detailed set of instructions about screenplay layout here, mainly because it can all be done for you nowadays using widely available software packages. The most well known package is **Final Draft**, which adheres to all industry standard layout guidelines. But it's not free – and it's actually not that cheap. Another one, slowly taking over the market, is **Celtx**. And this *is* free. The BBC also has one – **Script Smart** – which comes with a really handy instruction guide for laying out a screenplay, written as a screenplay itself. All of these packages – and others – are easy to use and allow you to save your documents in formats that others can open, such as Microsoft Word and PDF.

Nevertheless, I'll point out here a few guiding principles about laying out a screenplay:

- A **slugline**, or **scene heading**, indicates where a scene's set, which is necessary for both reading and production purposes. INT. means interior, or inside, and EXT. means exterior, or outside. The slugline also indicates a general idea of the time, such as morning, day, evening or night. Occasionally, screenwriters will give specific times.

- **Scene action**, or **screen directions**, details what's actually happening on the screen. It's used to describe both what we see and what we hear, and is always written in the present tense. Scene action is divided into short paragraphs, each paragraph usually not exceeding three or four lines. Scene action can also be just a word or two.

- The **character's name** indicates who's speaking, and written underneath this is their **dialogue**. A character sometimes speaks in voiceover, and this is still written as dialogue, with 'voiceover' or 'v/o' in parentheses next to, or underneath, the character's name.

- **Parentheses** are used when the screenwriter wants to indicate how something's said, if it's not clear from the dialogue. They're also used when a character performs a minor action between his or her lines, stopping the need to write scene action and break up the flow.

- Occasionally, **scene transitions** are written at the end of a scene to suggest how one scene moves into the next. But this is usually only for specific effect. The start of a new scene (slugline) implies a cut between scenes anyway. 'Cut to' can be used, but isn't necessary.

Here's an example of how a screenplay might look:

```
EXT. FOREST - NIGHT

It's quiet. And dark. Very dark. Even the
moonlight struggles to pierce the density of
the forest.

It's very still. Until…

All of a sudden, an animal darts past us.

No sooner is it here than it is gone.
Stillness once more.

INT. FOREST CABIN - NIGHT

Harris and Jordan drink beer in front of a
roaring fire. They just stare into the flames.

All of a sudden, the cuckoo clock strikes…
scaring the hell out of them both.

                    HARRIS
                 Jeez… !

Jordan laughs.
```

                    JORDAN
          Scared by the time of night, eh?!

                    HARRIS
                   (shaken)
          Those things are so frickin'
          creepy.

Jordan glances over to the clock, shaking his
head.

Harris finishes the rest of his beer, then
takes another one from the cooler. He offers
one to Jordan.

                    JORDAN
          Got a better idea.

                    HARRIS
          Too early for the chasers, man.

Jordan puts his bottle down and leans in
towards Harris. He grins.

                    JORDAN
          How about a nice walk?

Harris laughs, but seeing that Jordan's deadly
serious, suddenly looks horrified.

FORM

There are two things to consider when thinking about form. Firstly, screenwriting as a form – what does it mean to write a screenplay, and does that shape the writing process? As mentioned above, screenwriting is like no other form of creative writing. It does have similarities, of course, but it also has its own distinguishing features. The dominant vessel for telling the story is usually imagery, complemented by dialogue and driven by a central character, sometimes multiple central characters. The currency of screenwriting, although it's a visual medium, is structure. When people talk about screenplays, they talk about what happens. Common parlance involves plot points, inciting incidents, climaxes, resolutions and character arcs. Although these are important in all forms of writing, in screenwriting it's much more common to plan these things down to their fine detail. In fact, some screenwriters work on planning the screenplay (treatment, step outline) for months, even years, so that everyone understands how it's going to work. More often than not, the screenplay won't even be written. Or it might be written, but it won't have been commissioned. Some screenwriters make good careers out of selling story ideas. They dream of seeing their work on the screen, of course, but they spend years developing and selling outlines, treatments and step outlines.

Screenwriting is also a highly collaborative form, where everyone and their assistant will have ideas and notes. There's a lot at stake in screenwriting, especially feature films, most notably money. Everyone wants to make sure there's a good return. So, with that, everyone wants to make sure the story works – or at least ticks the boxes they think will make it work. Collaboration can begin with a screenwriter and producer developing an idea together, and can end with re-writes on the day of filming. In between, a whole host of notes can come from developers, financiers, script editors, executive producers, even actors. There's also the screenplay re-writer – the person or people brought in and paid to re-write sections of the screenplay, or the whole of it. There's a career to be had just doing this! It's more common than people think, and certainly more common than people know, because re-writers aren't often credited. Or, the re-writer gets the whole credit – and the original writer gets nothing (apart from payment). It's certainly a minefield, and not a form of writing for the faint-hearted. There are extremes, of course, and not every project will have this many people involved. But it's something to be aware of. Especially if you're transitioning from writing short stories and novels, where your words are your art and there's a lot less interference. Paul Ashton has a really useful chapter on screenwriting form in his book, *The Calling Card Script: A Writer's Toolbox for Screen, Stage and Radio* (2011). It's well worth a read, if not to give you new insights, then to clarify in your mind exactly how different writing forms – in this case, scriptwriting – are conceived and executed.

Secondly, there's the idea of what specific screenplay form your story should be told in. In other words, is your idea feature-film material or short-film gold? Or does your story lend itself better to television, as a series (continuing) or serial (closed)? Increasingly, is there scope for your story to work across different forms? Maybe you start with a feature, but you follow it up with a series of short films or webisodes? Or perhaps you start with webisodes that develop your central characters and their backstories, then feed these into a feature film? The whole cross-platform concept is complex and challenging – yet very exciting – and there's no space to talk about it here, I'm afraid. But it's definitely something you should think about if you've got a story idea that has many potential avenues of exploration – spin-offs, audience interaction, multi-threaded narratives, etc.

Here are some things to think about when deciding on your specific screenplay form:

- **Short films** tend to explore one event or an emotion, yet with great magnitude. They're tightly focused and, although they do have a narrative arc, may not have obvious or explicit beginnings, middles and ends.

- **Short films** can also be more experimental, playing around with shape, style and pace. Because they're short, they don't run the risk of losing their audience.

- **Feature films** tend to be much bigger in scale – not just length – exploring emotions and themes through various characters and situations. They're still tightly focused, but have a more expansive narrative and wider palette of characters, worlds, themes and subplots. They can be experimental, but, in the main, tend to follow traditional story structures and audience-friendly styles. Even 'alternative structures' are becoming mainstream, no longer feeling experimental and niche.

- **Television series and serials** tend to explore greater numbers of central characters in much more depth. Whether told over six, thirteen or twenty-six hours per year, the stories have a greater number of beats (physical and emotional advances) and often weave together many character journeys from the same story world.

Choosing the right form is crucial, both for yourself (developing the idea) and others (pitching the idea). There's nothing worse than spending weeks or months on an idea for a feature, only to be told that it's worth about 15 minutes of screen time. Or writing a short film that's really just a trailer for a feature – setting up lots of dramatic questions and webs of character relationships, rather than saying something meaningful and with a focused cast in the time allotted. It might sound strange, the idea of getting confused between a feature and a short, but it happens a lot. I've seen people passionately pitch their feature ideas, only to be told that what they've just described as the story will only take about five minutes of screen time. Lots of detail doesn't mean lots of story – lots of *story* means lots of story. I've also read quite a few short films that just didn't work in their own right, but did set up a world, a cast of characters and dramatic questions that would make a brilliant feature. Someone listening to such a pitch or reading such a screenplay might not take too kindly to having their time 'wasted' by your not having grasped the most basic of points. Something good may come of it – a professional rapport, advice for re-shaping the idea, etc – but that's only if the person listening or reading is kind. Otherwise, you may have blown your chance.

Watching an array of short films can really help to distinguish between forms. Good short films aren't always easy to find, but websites like YouTube, Shooting People, The Smalls, the BBC Film Network and Australian Short Films are increasingly showcasing brilliant work. And, of course, short film festivals – a great way to see what's being made and what works. I recently attended two events at the Australian Centre for the Moving Image, and saw a collection of original, powerful short films about wartime death, children and immigration, the pressure to please and what it's like being a drag queen in Cuba. They all worked because their stories suited the form – and they couldn't have been anything else.

If you're having trouble finding your form – especially whether or not your idea has enough fuel and appeal to be a feature – you might find some of the structural models offered in Chapter 6 useful. These models, along with the accompanying discussion of them, should give you a better idea of the amount of story and how big a controlling idea you'll need.

Creative exercise

Using the title *Lost and Found*, come up with an idea for a short film of five minutes' duration. Now come up with another idea, using the same title, this time for a short film lasting ten minutes. What's changed? Is it a new idea, or based on the shorter one? How many more characters have you added? Now come up with an idea for a feature, using the same title. How has this changed? What does it tell you about the parameters of screenplay form?

A FILM ABOUT SCREENWRITING

A useful – and fun – film to watch that explores the nature of screenwriting is *Adaptation* (scr. Charlie Kaufman & Donald Kaufman, 2002). This is a film about a screenwriter – Charlie Kaufman – and his attempts to adapt a book written by Susan Orlean. It works on so many levels – his attempts to adapt a book that we see her writing, his twin brother's attempts to also become a screenwriter, the character of screenwriting guru Robert McKee, etc – that, for a screenwriter, it's actually a great insight into what it's like to write. The irony of the film is that Charlie's trying his hardest to get away from the usual structure-driven methods of screenwriting and instead find the theme of the book that he's trying to adapt – the meaning that can drive the creation of his screenplay. All the while, his brother's foray into screenwriting is epitomised by everything he's trying to avoid. Donald talks about inciting incidents and act turning points, and even attends a Robert McKee seminar. There's a scene that visualises this dilemma – the dilemma of the screenwriter, not just the relationship of these brothers – really well. We see both Charlie and Donald in the same room, reading. But whereas Charlie's reading the book he's trying to adapt, *The Orchid Thief*, Donald's reading McKee's book, *Story*. It's a nice nod to the screenwriter in the audience.

What's really interesting about this film is how the energy changes around the end of the second act, linked to the brothers' preoccupations. As soon as Charlie invites Donald to New York to help him track down Susan, the film becomes much more like a 'standard' Hollywood film – everything that Donald epitomises. So, whereas Charlie is seeking help so that he can get the real meaning of the book from Susan, Donald arrives and totally changes the dynamic of what we're watching. We go from thinking about themes and the inherent problems of the characters to espionage, car chases and, eventually, dramatic deaths. As a screenwriter, then, it's really interesting to see this shift in the film's pace and tone, and work out what it means for the character of the screenwriter, Charlie. In one way, Donald's arrival destroys the story – it turns dark, and two characters get killed. In another way, however, Donald's arrival helps the story: through the structure now imposed on the characters, both Charlie and Susan – the main protagonists – find their emotional arc, which is what Charlie's been contemplating from the start. So structure – through the character of Donald – is both a friend and a foe. It moves the story on, but also destroys two of the people in the story. And it's questions like this, raised through the complex, intertextual layers of the film, that make *Adaptation* a must-see for any aspiring or working screenwriter.

2. FINDING IDEAS

A good place to start when thinking about ideas for screenplays is to look both outside and inside of yourself. In other words, it's about considering what's happening around you (socially, culturally, economically, politically), and what's happening within you (emotionally, psychologically). When you put these two things together – processing events happening around you into internal thoughts and feelings – you've got theme and meaning. Then, when you put all that into screenplay form – characters, world, plot, etc – you've got storytelling. And that's why, as a species, we love stories: because they tell us about the world we live in, and through a lens we understand (the human perspective).

Michael Rabiger's book, *Developing Story Ideas* (2005), asks its readers to think about the stories they want – and are able – to tell. In other words, what he's getting at it is that, as a writer, you should take time to think about what you know and how that might be something that others want to know, too. You might think that you don't know anything – or at least anything new or different – but that's simply not true. Of course you know something. And although it might not be radical or different on the surface, it's new and exciting in that it's something seen through you – it's your perspective. Take the following, for example:

- Love
- Hatred
- Forgiveness
- Marriage
- Family
- Death

Your view on, or interpretation of, these things is different to mine. And your partner's. And your neighbour's. When you have a conversation about these things – or any things, really – with other people, what you say will be interesting to them. And what they say will be interesting to you – even if you don't agree with their views. That's because each and every one of us has an insight that's interesting to someone else. We all have insights. Therefore, we all have ideas. An elaborate, blow-away plot or a unique, multi-dimensional protagonist can be developed and crafted around an idea. But if the idea isn't there in the first place, these components will struggle to find intention and meaning.

Creative exercise
Using one of the words from the list above, write a stream-of-conscious monologue (automatic writing) about your views on the subject. Don't hold back. Just write. Tell yourself what you think about it. Bring in any experiences you have of it. Be as judgemental as you like. When you've done that, step away from it and try to boil down your thoughts into a sentence or two. What's your 'manifesto' on the subject? And how might you translate that into a character and a plot?

SOURCING IDEAS

It can be useful – especially if you really can't find anything to write about – to look around you for story triggers. Hopefully you'll find something you really want to write about, and so these triggers will be a mere exercise in being creative and trying to come up with good ideas. But you may find that you work better when you're given the starting point for an idea – the job then being to create characters, themes, a world and a story structure from it. It doesn't matter where you get your ideas, really – and you'll probably find that ideas merge, fuse and change all the time. What does matter is that you can begin to work with an idea, and make it something more than it currently is.

Here are some examples of common – and fun – ways of getting ideas for screenplays. Each one is followed by a key consideration, so you can start to hone your skills in sourcing and developing ideas from each:

- **Newspaper headlines** – they can be catchy ('Text sex pest doesn't get message') and emotive ('Woman loses mother and child in accident'). They usually give you a vague sense of plot, character and tone, and the starting point for a world. What you usually need to develop is theme and structure.

- **Photographs** – either personal or from a magazine, TV, website, etc, they can give a strong sense of theme and character. Because they usually depict a real person and/or event, memory comes into play quite strongly. They work well with film because they could be the basis for an actual scene or shot.

- **Objects** – pick an object and start writing about it. It could be an object you know, or something you see randomly. Forcing yourself to write about it makes you think about its qualities – personality, use, history, worth, etc. Though a fun exercise, it might actually give you an idea – such as an important object that a character possesses.

- **Eavesdropping** – this can be fun, if done properly – and ethically. Listen out for what people are talking about, and how they're talking about it. It can often give you a really strong sense of character, through attitude and point-of-view. What you'd need to think about is how these ideas turn into a plot – what actually happens to bring this voice out?

- **Music** – there's something really emotive about music, which is a great way of immersing yourself in thinking about the world, and it's bound to give you ideas. You might use the actual words of a song as fuel for an idea, but it'll be the emotion created by the score that connects with you. It might give you ideas for themes and worlds, which you can create characters and plots for.

- **History** – whether personal or national/global, reading about history can be fruitful. You might find an 'angle' that nobody's explored, like someone's alternate view of something that happened, or a hidden piece of information. Here, you usually try to find a new character and/or theme – a different perspective on something we already know about.

- **Automatic writing** – just writing – with no bounds – forces you to say something, which might eventually morph into a solid idea. Your brain works overtime, frantically trying to make something out of nothing – such as starting each new sentence with the next letter of the alphabet. It might create interesting dramatic combinations you hadn't considered before.

Whenever you see, hear or feel a story, keep it tucked away somewhere. You might want to come back to it another day, either as the starting point for a new story, or to inject into something you're already writing. You might also find yourself in a situation where you're being asked for your next idea – by a producer, for example – so it's always worth having a bank of them somewhere. You might even work these ideas up to synopsis or outline stage, just in case – see Chapters 3 and 12 for further details.

WHAT'S IN AN IDEA?

An idea is only an idea when it's got a future – when it's got the potential to go somewhere. Otherwise, it's just a fact – just a 'thing'. An idea suggests intention – something that resides in the 'thing' that's got the potential to become something else. In our case, it's a musing about a character or a plot or a theme or a world that will eventually become a screenplay. Because our ideas are intended for other people – an audience – they need to have something that's going to be of interest, and going to connect with them. Sometimes this is clear from the start. At other times, it's going to take the advice of someone in the development process to help you. Either way, your idea needs to have something appealing in it that will warrant the film being made. And a good thing to consider here is its universal appeal. In other words, what's in your idea that others are going to want to hear about, and possibly share? How will your screenplay create an emotional connection with its intended audience? Or, to use a well-worn phrase, how is art going to imitate life?

This is where it's useful to ask, what's in the zeitgeist? What are people talking about at the minute? What are society's concerns? These are useful questions to ask because, essentially, you're trying to reach out to people's emotions and get them to see what you're trying to say. Even in comedy, which might not be emotional in its appeal, there's a sense that something's funny in context. In other words, people laugh at the jokes because they mean something in relation to what they know. Satire and parody are obvious forms of comedy here – the laughs coming from a point of comparison between the joke and the context (political, social, cultural, etc). Ideas also have to work for the world and the characters of your screenplay – their zeitgeist. What's being explored in your story might not necessarily tap into the specific consciousness of the people you're writing for – though, arguably, it should certainly tap into their emotions – but it should tap into the consciousness of the people you're writing about. This makes your screenplay feel real and true.

Films can easily fall down because they don't feel relevant to our world or the characters' world. *Weekend* (scr. Andrew Haigh, 2011) is an example of such a film – although its execution was strong, with great performances and some wonderful dialogue, thematically it's very dated. The world it's trying to convey – a contemporary Britain that still has major hang-ups about homosexuality – just doesn't feel true. Worse still, the central character of Glen feels like he belongs in the 1970s, not the second decade of the twenty-first century. His entire arc centres around a deep need to prove to the world that gay people can live normal lives – a need so profound that he moves to America where he can be free and accepted. But it just doesn't feel right. It jars, emotionally, because it feels like a world that no longer exists. Similarly, *Any Questions For Ben* (scr. Santo Cilauro, Tom Gleisner & Rob Sitch, 2012) feels really inappropriate for its characters. The film explores ideas of self-worth, social value and missed chances – all of which would suit a mid-life crisis type of situation. But the protagonist, Ben, is 27, and practically all of his friends are around the same age. What's worse is that Ben declares his love for Alex, telling her that he regrets never getting to know her at university, and how he remembers watching her in the canteen in between lectures, and how he was enamoured of her. But because, at 27, he's likely to have left university only five or six years before, it feels very contrived and convenient rather than credible and true. If the central characters were shaped around the film's core themes, making the world of the story much more believable, then the film might have been much more successful – critically and commercially. So it's really important when developing an idea to allow time for the story to find its own shape and a voice that speaks both to its audience and its characters.

KNOWING WHEN AN IDEA'S READY

The more you can let an idea gestate, the stronger it's likely to be. Sometimes we make quick judgements and decisions, but it's only when we let them brew for a while and come back to them that they find their own way and, in screenwriting, feel more original and true. So if you can let an idea breathe and morph, you might feel happier with what you're writing.

For example, imagine seeing someone run into the street and get killed by an oncoming car. The shock of seeing it might spur you on to write. And it's that shock that's likely to be driving you. Your mind might be racing with ideas – who was this person? why did they run into the street? who was driving? – but they're likely to be coming from the same place. But, if you let the idea percolate, you'll think about the event differently, and might find a better story. For example, was it an accident, or did they mean to run in front of the oncoming car? Did the runner know the driver? Was it a set-up? How is the driver now feeling? Is there an interesting reason why the driver was there at that exact time? And what about the witnesses? Who saw the accident? How has it affected their life? What about the people who have to come and clean up the accident? What do they think when they arrive? Why do they do that job? Is it well paid? Or do they long to do something else? The ideas are endless and, as you can see from these questions, the more you let an idea find its own form, spinning in different directions and testing different waters, the more original – or at least less clichéd – it will become. And that's what a good screenwriter does – finds an interesting and fresh angle to something we all know.

Creative exercise

Take the situation described above and come up with ten different story ideas. Keep asking questions – like above – to push the ideas as far as they'll go and to find original ideas. If you like, summarise each of your ten ideas in a short paragraph – no more than 250 words.

Don't underestimate the power of letting an idea sit for a while. It can be frustrating if you've got a great idea and it's not quite working – of course – but if you try and force it out, it's likely that you'll end up with a bad idea and a bad screenplay. Instead, give it time – and if it's a great idea that you truly believe in, it'll come and get you when it's ready. You might have a pressing deadline, which can be a nightmare. But, if you plan ahead and schedule in time for leaving the idea alone for a while, you'll not panic and ruin it. Also, having other ideas to work on is a really great way of helping the problem idea come to fruition. Whether this is to distract you from the pain of trying to make it work, or as a way of exploring something that's not working – such as not being able to get the voice of your protagonist – what it'll do is provide some much-needed creative space where your problem idea can float for a while until it's ready to be tackled again. In this case, don't rush your new idea as a way of trying to get back to the problem idea as quickly as you can – take your time and have fun with the new idea, allowing it to organically breathe new life into the idea that's stuck.

Finally, it can be really useful to read how other writers find and develop ideas. Although everyone works differently, there are common themes – recognising when an idea's good, first steps to developing that idea, probing and expanding the idea, knowing when the idea's running out of steam, etc. Graeme Harper's book, *Inside Creative Writing: Interviews with Contemporary Writers* (2012), asks a host of practising writers about the processes they go through when writing creatively. A book like this can be both insightful and inspiring. Kevin Conroy Scott's *Screenwriters' Masterclass* (2005) and Alistair Owen's *Story and Character* (2004) present a range of interviews with screenwriters, and are really useful for understanding how writers work. The *Backstory* series of books – edited by Patrick McGilligan – are also a good read.

3. DEVELOPING IDEAS

There's no single way to develop an idea. We all work differently, depending on our individual preferences and industry circumstances, and so our approach to developing a screenplay will be individual – and it might change from project to project. This can be both an advantage and a disadvantage. On the one hand, who wants to work in the same way as everyone else? Who wants to follow strictures and be told how to do things? Some of us prefer to work on structure first, and then character – and only theme at the very end. Some of us prefer to start with theme, and from that let characters develop, and only structure at the very end. Whilst some of us work within formal parameters – chronologically, linearly – some of us work in layers, to keep digging deeper and discovering.

On the other hand, who wants to jeopardise their chances of getting a screenplay read – or made – because they haven't yet worked up something that a producer or director wants – outline, treatment, character profiles, first draft, etc? Some of us prefer to knock out a first draft as quickly as possible, so there's something concrete to work on and use as a sample should the opportunity arise. Some of us prefer to nail the structure first, spending a long time developing a treatment or step outline so that we're confident the story's going to work. The actual screenplay can come later.

But what if a producer or director wants to see an extensive treatment first, and you haven't got one? Or if they want to read the screenplay first, to get a sense of your voice, but you haven't started it? It can be a tricky predicament to be in. Sometimes you might be able to convince them that what you've got is appropriate; other times you might need to find out what they're likely to want before you start developing. If you're going to enter competitions then at least the guidelines are set – they want a five-page treatment and a one-page synopsis, for example – but even then, if you're lucky enough to get to the next stage, they might want something else from you that you might or might not have got.

WHERE TO START?

Although aimed at people working in advertising, I find Nik Mahon's *Basics Advertising 03: Ideation* (2011) extremely useful for teaching people how to develop creative ideas. Some of the processes a screenwriter goes through are much the same as an advertiser coming up with a new campaign – or in fact anyone working in creative development. The basic premise is this – open yourself up to possibilities. If you approach with a closed mind, thinking that your idea's already perfect, then it's possible your screenplay's going to be fairly unoriginal and uninspiring. If, instead, you allow your imagination to roam free, and for ideas to grow and die, it's more likely that you'll end up with a more original and refreshing screenplay. This was the premise behind Zara Waldeback and I writing *The Creative Screenwriter*, in fact – a plea for screenwriters to embrace creativity during the development process, so as not to lock in ideas too early.

Mahon talks about divergent and convergent thinking as a way of starting to embrace creativity in the development process. Here's a summary, which I've related to screenwriting:

- **Divergent thinking** – thinking outside the box and looking in all directions for alternative ideas. It's about letting go of boundaries, logic and reasoning, and playing with these new ideas to see if they actually bring anything that's useable –

and fresh. For example, what if your story was set in the past rather than the present? What if your protagonist was a serial killer as well as a schoolteacher? What if your antagonist was gay instead of straight? What if you switched from a horror to a comedy? What if the world of your story doesn't allow people to talk about sex?

- **Convergent thinking** – evaluating the ideas that have come out of divergent thinking, and assessing their viability. It's about refocusing on the problem at hand – how to develop your screenplay – and trying to match crazy ideas with story credibility. From the random ideas you've had, is there potential in there for something to actually work? Has being creative opened up story possibilities? Has the seed been planted for doing something truly original?

He also talks about the process of ideation, and how, as a creative, you go through four key stages when developing an idea – preparation (brainstorming, fact finding, sampling), incubation (gestating, relaxing, reflecting), illumination (realising, capturing, producing) and verification (evaluating, critiquing, re-working). I've taken these steps as the basis for what I'm calling the 5 Ps process – steps for a screenwriter to develop their idea:

- **Ploughing** – using story triggers that work for you, listening, observing, thinking, living, playing, experimenting and researching.

- **Processing** – building ideas into characters, plots and themes, finding a form, developing a structure, designing a cast, writing and finding out.

- **Pruning** – going back to the work and re-shaping, making further decisions about structure, cast, voice, style and tone, and re-drafting.

- **Pitching** – pitching as telling, not just selling, wanting and needing feedback, understanding your idea and seeing it differently.

- **Polishing** – re-writing after feedback, re-visiting screenwriting craft and honing.

Creative exercise

Think about the last screenplay that you wrote – or the one you're currently writing – and write down specific details about how you developed the idea. Try to remember as much as you can – no matter how small. Then assign each thing from your list to one of the 5 Ps above. When you've assigned them all, see which 'P' has the most. Are there any glaring gaps or imbalances? What does this tell you about your development process?

INDUSTRY INSIGHT

Zara Waldeback, a Swedish-based writer and director of short dramas and features, and co-author of *Writing for the Screen: Creative and Critical Approaches* and *The Creative Screenwriter: Exercises to Expand Your Craft*, has this to say:

Welcoming the unexpected

Hopefully we set out with some sort of plan when writing a screenplay. This is a very good idea, as structure, intention and focus are a big part of creating a strong and successful story. But it's never the whole story. Whether you like it or not, there's always a degree of mystery involved when writing – or directing – a film. Something will happen that's unexpected, maybe wildly so – a character suddenly reveals another side, the plot takes a different turn, a world falls away and is replaced, you realise you really want to write about something else, etc. What do you do?

Sometimes you have to say 'no, thanks, this isn't for this story' because, even though it's a good idea, it doesn't fit and would change the script too much. But often it's useful to open the door to the unexpected and see what it has to tell you. For me, writing is a delight and a joy because it's so much about exploring the unknown. I never feel I make up a story completely, but rather that the story reveals itself to me if I listen to it and pay attention. When unexpected moments come along, I try to walk along with them for a while to see where they will lead me – then I'll decide if it's the right path or not.

When I write, I don't always want to stay in control. I want to allow the story to push and pull me, blow me like the wind into far-flung territories where I might get a bit nervous or scared – how will I get out of here? At the same time, when I re-write or edit or analyse a draft, I do want to have control – I want to know what it is I'm trying to write, how and if it's being expressed, how to improve it. For me, writing is a dance between allowing myself to be free with the story so it transports me to strange and wondrous places, and coming back home with little gems that I sort through to see where they fit. Then I go out on another adventure, come home and sort through, etc. This process means I'm open to things I've not thought of, and these can be places where magic happens. Without that, I think the story could be dry and half-dead – neatly laid out and perfectly manicured – but not vibrating with life. Writing screenplays is about touching someone, making an impact, creating a reaction. It's not about staying small, playing it safe.

A small story to illustrate my point, which shows that welcoming the unexpected is just as important when it comes to directing films as it is when you're writing them. When I directed my first big-budget short film, I'd done weeks of planning and preparation. I'd gone through every word of the script – created a myriad of questions, ideas, suggestions, motivations, possibilities. I had a thick notebook full of ideas about how to direct scenes, moments and meetings. Then, on the first day of the week-long shoot, I lost it – my precious notebook with all my brilliant ideas, gone! I had no choice but to plough on without it. It forced me to stay in the moment, pay attention to what was happening in front of me, and not hang on to what I'd planned in my head. When the shoot ended and we were tidying up the van, I found the book nestled behind some cushions in the seating area. It had been there all along. I realised then that, if I'd had my notebook with me, I would've been glued to it instead of being present with the story unfolding in front of me.

But – and here's the crucial part – if I'd not done all that careful, thoughtful preparation beforehand, I wouldn't have been able to work spontaneously in such a successful, confident and informed way. I'd done my homework and given myself the tools I needed to travel well in the unknown. I realised that, when telling stories, I can't hold on only to what I know – I have to go further. But I don't do so unprepared or unequipped – I do all I can so I'm clear and focused and ready. And it's then that I know I'll be able to enjoy and delight in welcoming the unexpected – and let my stories come fully alive.

© Zara Waldeback, 2012

DEVELOPMENT DOCUMENTS

As you develop your screenplay, you might want to try working with one or more development documents. They can help you to thrash out your idea in full, find narrative focus, experiment with structure, test out character arcs, clarify theme – and much more. There's sometimes an overlap between a development document and a selling document – such as a treatment – but in this chapter I'm going to focus on the ones that mainly help you to work on your screenplay, not sell it. Selling documents will be discussed in Chapter 12.

Before I go into detail about some of the documents used in development, it's worth reiterating that there's no one-size-fits-all. Although there are common principles that most people abide by, you might find different nuances between producers, directors, script developers, competitions, funding schemes, etc. Some of these can be very minor – such as layout and font – but some can be bigger, such as level of detail and style of language. What I'll be discussing here are the most common principles found in development documents.

Whichever document you want to work with, it should try and do the following:

- Capture the key structural elements (what happens?)
- Capture the key themes (what's it about?)
- Capture the imagination of the reader (why should they be interested?)
- Capture the style and tone of the screenplay, and its intended audience (who's going to want to watch this?)

It's also useful to keep track of the development of both the protagonist's physical journey and emotional journey – see Chapter 6 for more detail on this. Or, to put it another way, keep reminding yourself of the Central Dramatic Question (CDQ) – what happens? – and the Central Thematic Question (CTQ) – why should we care? By doing this, you'll not lose sight of why you're telling the story, and you'll know what the structure's supposed to be achieving.

You might first want to develop a **sequence outline**. This is a short document – usually only a couple of pages – that gives a condensed overview of the complete story broken down into its key sequences, which is usually eight – again, see Chapter 6 for more detail on this. You construct the sequence outline by describing each sequence in a short paragraph, considering its beginning, middle and end. In other words, you're summarising each sequence as if it's a short film in itself, with its own three-act structure. You might occasionally be asked for a sequence outline, but usually it's only a working document for you. You can also construct the sequence outline by referring to other structural models, such as Christopher Vogler's 12-step Hero's Journey. What the sequence outline does is give you a clear sense of the key plot points in your screenplay, and how they play out, one after the other.

For some screenwriters, the next task is to write a **step outline**, sometimes also known as a **scene-by-scene**. This is a fairly bare-bones document, which can be short or actually quite long, and which maps out the story in separate units or scenes. It gives brief descriptions of each step of the story – usually only a couple of sentences – telling only its major action and/or emotion (physical journey and emotional journey). A step outline allows you to see the map of the screenplay and work out where the key turning points are. Because they're usually written in the same font as a screenplay – complete with scene headings – some screenwriters actually build their screenplay from the step outline. This can make the development process coherent and feel integrated (idea with screenplay). Another way of mapping out the steps of your story is by using index cards. Again, you just write a couple of sentences about each step – one card per step – and then you can shuffle them around to play with the structure.

The other big development document – that can be, and often is, used for pitching – is the **treatment**. This is a longer document that tells the complete story in fulsome, polished prose. It's a longer version of the outline (see Chapter 12), giving much more attention to detail. In fact, it's much like a short-story version of the screenplay. A treatment can range from anything between 5 and 35 pages – it all depends on what the writer needs and, if using it to sell the screenplay, what the producer (or other) wants. A treatment is written in the present tense, the action playing out for the reader. It should be broken down into short, concise paragraphs, and the language should be considered carefully to give a texture, flavour and tone that in some way mirrors what would be the experience of seeing the film. If it's a comedy, make it funny. If it's a thriller, make it thrilling. Key snatches of dialogue may be included, if necessary – a key phrase or line, for example; otherwise it's normal for a treatment to be written purely in prose.

Creative exercise

Have a go at writing one of the above development documents for someone else's screenplay. It might be someone that you know, or it might be a produced film. It doesn't matter which – the idea is for you to start thinking analytically about how a screenplay works by summarising it. Don't worry if you can't capture all the details – broad brushstrokes is fine. Just make sure that you write in the style of the document you've chosen – as detailed above – and that you start to understand the story more clearly by writing it out.

How – and with whom – you work on these development documents depends on your position in the industry and your writing habits. If you've got a commission, then a producer or script editor might want to see these documents at various stages, giving you feedback and helping you to hone them. If you're using them as part of a competition, or a funding or mentoring scheme, then it's likely that you'll be asked for a shorter one in the first instance, so the assessors can get a flavour of your idea. Then, through progressive development, you might be asked for a bigger one, until you're ready to write a draft of the screenplay.

If you're working alone, with a writing partner, or in a writing circle, you might be less formal about what you construct, seeing it as more of a prompt than an official document that has ramifications for other people. Either way, development documents can be really useful for taking a step back from your screenplay and understanding – or trying to work out – what's going on. If you're stuck on something, such as a flawed structure or a two-dimensional character, chances are that working on a development document will help you. Sometimes they're a hard slog to write, and they take you away from the fun of writing the actual screenplay – but when done well, they're certainly worth the effort.

4. CREATING A WORLD

Creating a compelling and convincing world is one of the most important elements of screenwriting. However, it's one of the least talked about. I think many screenwriting authors and teachers see it as a given – that a world will be built organically when the screenplay's written. Or that it's a simple part of the screenwriting process – it's just about creating believability, and doesn't really need to be thought about too much. Although elements of this aren't wrong, there's so much more to say about worlds. A world is infectious – it affects all other elements of your screenplay, from story to character to dialogue. It doesn't just hold your screenplay together, it pulls and pushes it into shape. In fact, world is something that can easily make or break your screenplay.

A well-chosen and well-crafted world can create a specific audience experience – a particular tone and feeling that the plot can't convey by itself. A world also has its own innate dramatic potential, where your choice can both help and hinder how the story's told. A world can belong to a particular character, too, and by imposing a new world on that character – or bringing a new character into their world – you can create interesting, dramatic challenges that they have to work with. A well-chosen world can also bring a familiar, clichéd story alive again, making it feel fresh and inspiring. Many successful films take a classic storyline and set it in a new, sometimes unusual, world. This helps to make the story feel new and exciting, and relevant for a contemporary audience. Examples include *Pretty Woman* (scr. JF Lawton, 1990), *Enchanted* (scr. Bill Kelly, 2007), *Pan's Labyrinth* (*El Laberinto del Fauno*) (scr. Guillermo del Toro, 2006) and *Million Dollar Baby* (scr. Paul Haggis, 2004).

So, creating a world means far more than creating a location for the story to take place in. Location comes into it, clearly, but a screenplay world is also about:

- The feel of the story – how does the world affect the tone of what we're seeing?

- Internal logic – how does the world operate?

- The emotional experience of the audience – how is it brought about by the world?

- A vessel for theme and meaning – what stories are able to be told in this world?

- Voicing a script – does the world have its own voice, attitude and perspective?

Paris, Je T'aime (scr. Various, 2006) is a film about a world – a collection of 18 short films that celebrate the city of Paris. Taking as its frame one Parisian arrondissement per short film, the collection, as a whole, explores what it's like to live in Paris, amongst all of its beauty and disparity. The central theme is love – Paris as the city of love, and also why we love Paris (hence the title). As such, although each short film has its own story world – a comedy mime, a lascivious vampire, a grieving family, etc – the feature film (compilation) draws its components together to explore a single world – contemporary Paris, where there's something for everyone.

> **Creative exercise**
> Choose a film and consider what world – or worlds – it presents. Where is it set? How does the world operate? What's the feel of the world? How does this world – unlike others – enable themes to be explored and meaning to come about? Are there any specific characteristics of the world, such as character types, voice/dialogue and visual motifs? Overall, how potent is the world of this film? Could the film exist in another world?

BUILDING YOUR WORLD

When developing your story, you should spend as much time as possible building your world. As I've already highlighted, it can be something that makes or breaks your screenplay – not just in the sense of appealing to the right producer or director, but also in the sense that it can open up your story to fresh and exciting possibilities. Spending time on your world can really strengthen your screenplay in ways that you might not expect – characters, structure, themes, dialogue, etc. Here, then, I want to talk briefly about some of the ways that you can build your story world – things that you should consider as you're working on all other essential elements of your screenplay. As I've already stated, a story world is infectious – it can dominate your screenplay in many ways. The case studies below will explore some of these ideas in more detail.

When **casting the world** – working out who you need to tell your story – you need to think carefully about the composition of characters. The protagonist will belong to a specific world, then is likely to be transported to another world, either literally or metaphorically. So you need to know what these worlds are, and how they work for the story. It's the same for the antagonist – what world do they want to destroy or control, and how does this fit with their situation and personality? You need to think about supporting characters, too, and what they might bring to or from the story world. Questions you should consider include:

- Which characters belong in the world?

- Which characters don't belong in the world?

- When characters that don't belong in the world still inhabit it, how do they and other characters react?

- What are the character hierarchies of the world, and how are they maintained?

- What relationships exist between the characters and their world? How does the world affect them on a daily basis?

When you develop your screenplay's structure, you should consider the part the world plays in it. **Structuring the world** means finding the specific ways in which the world operates – internal logic included – and how these might dictate the structure that you use to tell your story. For example, your world might have rules that affect what characters can and can't do. Your structure will therefore be directly affected by this as your choices of character action are limited. You might decide that your world has a specific past or future – again, this will affect the structure of your screenplay because it means that certain things have already happened or will happen. The world, then, can have a real impact on your narrative structure. Questions you should consider include:

- Does the world have a specific, tangible hold on the plot – things that literally can or can't happen?

- Does the world suggest – or demand – a specific type of emotional movement or arc? What does the world do to people, and how does that trigger character arcs?

- What's the pace or feel of the world, and how does that play out in the sequences and scenes you write?

- Are actions affected by the world? What do characters feel they can and can't do?

- What different varieties or versions of the world exist, and how do they play out through the plot?

It can be surprising, yet illuminating, to think how dialogue can be influenced by the story world. It's about **voicing the world** – finding ways to verbally represent the world. There are sometimes really obvious demands on dialogue, such as technical jargon and words or expressions that belong to a specific world. A film set aboard a spaceship, for example, would require a specific way of speaking that relates to technology, situation and era. But voicing the world goes beyond this – it's about finding out how the world affects characters' attitudes, perspectives and topics of conversation. How would money-hungry stockbrokers talk on a night out? What would starving children talk to each other about? Questions you should consider include:

- What does the world sound like – does it have a universal voice?

- How might character dialogue be infected by the world – attitude, perspective, etc?

- Does the dialogue complement or in fact juxtapose the world?

- Is there a style and pace to character dialogue that reflects what the world's about?

- What are the competing voices in the world, and how do they go about being heard?

Theming the world is about understanding how the world you've chosen demands – or denies – that certain themes be explored. It's about knowing what stories need to be told, and what meaning an audience might be left with. Genre comes into play here because it can often dictate the theme of a story, or at least some kind of meaning that the audience is expecting. The world of a political thriller might demand themes of corruption and justice, for example. The world of a romantic comedy might demand themes of prejudice and narrow-mindedness. So, when building your world – and considering the genre of your story – you need to think about how specific themes naturally fit, or resist, it. Questions you should consider include:

- Does the world demand a type of understanding that translates into an obvious theme?

- Which themes are already prevalent in the world, and which are denied?

- How might theme and meaning be woven into the world through characters, action, visual motifs and dialogue – and then communicated out again, to the audience?

INDUSTRY INSIGHT

Melbourne-based screenwriter, filmmaker and lecturer Annabelle Murphy, who convenes the screenwriting provision at the Victorian College of the Arts, has this to say:

Worlds that sing
Creating a rich and believable world for your story is a vital aspect of screenwriting. I believe that one hallmark of *all* great films, without exception, is a vivid and authentic world – not a setting, but a fully envisaged world. If that world is unique and largely unexplored in cinema, then so much the better. Take *The*

Godfather (scr. Mario Puzo & Francis Ford Coppola, 1972), *The Gods Must Be Crazy* (scr. Jamie Uys, 1980) and *My Life as a Dog* (scr. Lasse Hallstrom, Reidar Jonsson, Brasse Brannstrom & Per Berglund, 1985) as cases in point.

A vivid, authentic world brings depth and life to a film. Anyone who reads screenplays for a living will tell you that a film that 'knows what it is' and has a fresh authentic voice stands out from the crowd. The simplest way to achieve authenticity in portraying a film world is to know that world yourself. This is why autobiography is often so compelling. Real-life details and events are often so intriguingly specific that they couldn't easily be imagined by a writer, let alone portrayed with credibility.

But this isn't the only way. Many of our most loved film worlds are not 'real'. The *Harry Potter* series (2001–11), *Gattaca* (scr. Andrew Niccol, 1997), *Blade Runner* (scr. Hampton Fancher & David Peoples, 1982), *Groundhog Day* (scr. Danny Rubin & Harold Ramis, 1993) and so many more stories have been set in complex imaginary worlds painstakingly and lovingly realised by their screenwriters.

So, what makes one film world more compelling than another? For me, there's a triumvirate of qualities – for a film world to 'sing', it must be unique, vivid and authentic.

- **Unique** – think 'specific'. Never set your story in a 'generic' world because you think it'll make the story more accessible to a larger audience. This is the quickest path to mediocrity. Audiences respond to the specific and unique. *La Haine* (scr. Mathieu Kassovitz, 1995), *The Full Monty* (scr. Simon Beaufoy, 1997) and *Whale Rider* (scr. Niki Caro, 2002) work because they're set within highly specific worlds and cultures, which are intrinsic to the characters' psyches and the film's plot events.

- **Vivid** – think 'detail'. What are the colours, textures, sounds, buildings, food, plants, clothes and *so much more* of your world? A screenplay is by necessity concise and precise, so one skill of creating a vivid world on the page is to learn how much, and which, detail to put into a scene, and how much and what, to leave out. Carefully selected vivid detail enlivens a screenplay and evokes tone, character and world. Too much detail can kill it dead.

- **Authentic** – think 'internal logic'. Does the film make sense within its own parameters from the opening to the closing frame? Do the characters always behave believably? Are the physical, cultural and legal 'laws' of the world credibly portrayed? Note here the difference between 'truth' and 'internal logic' – a world or event doesn't need to be 'true' to feel authentic. Alternatively, 'truth' is no defence in a screenplay. If you can't make the 'truth' feel authentic, then it needs to be reworked.

© Annabelle Murphy, 2012

CASE STUDIES

The following case studies take a closer look at story world, and how each film uses the idea of a world to tell us something about itself – its characters, structure, theme, dialogue, etc.

Ratatouille (scr. Brad Bird, 2007) has two sets of internal logic to deal with. First of all, we have to understand that this is a world where rats can talk – and cook! From the start, we see rats Remy and Emile living an 'ordinary' life – they're scrounging around for food in an old lady's house, but at the same time making conversation, watching TV and joking about Remy's knowledge of cooking. This is important in setting up the logic that this is a film where rats have the characteristics and intelligence of humans – albeit unknown to humans themselves (until later). Animation helps with this too, of course. Remy finding himself in Paris is also important because it gives us a sense of reality – this is a place we know, and use of icons like the Eiffel Tower and the Arc de Triomphe also helps with this.

As the story develops, we then have to understand a new internal logic – that of Remy being able to 'control' rookie chef Linguini, and make him cook wonderful things. This is an important part of the story as it's what puts Linguini in jeopardy in the first place – because Remy can cook, and everyone else thinks it's Linguini, the challenge is set for Linguini to help restore the reputation of the restaurant. So, to show us this new internal logic, we see a 'training' sequence where Remy and Linguini figure out ways of working together – Remy controlling Linguini's arms for stirring, chopping, etc.

In *The Kids Are All Right* (scr. Lisa Cholodenko & Stuart Blumberg, 2010), we're presented with two distinct worlds: the 'perfect', upper-middle-class world of lesbian couple Nic and Jules and their two kids (beautiful house, academically-focused, good wine, etc), and the earthy, lower-middle-class world of the kids' biological father Paul (organic co-op farm, trendy restaurant, unplanned approach, etc). How this film works is seeing the transition of characters between the two worlds. For example, daughter Joni doesn't want to be part of this world (she doesn't want to meet Paul, their biological father), but son Laser does. This changes, though, after their first meeting with Paul – now it's Joni who wants to be part of his world and Laser not. Paralleling this, mother Nic wants nothing to do with Paul and his world – she's scared she'll lose control of her kids – whereas second mother Jules does want to be part of this new environment, and, by taking on a landscaping project for Paul, explores who she is – and wants to be. This is nicely symbolised by the metaphor of the garden that she's landscaping: a site that needs to be worked on, and new life given to it. Metaphorically, this represents Jules' own need for growth and 'work on the self'. In fact, when she first visits the garden, she says that they shouldn't try and tame it, that it should be fecund – fertile, able to grow, imaginative. Clearly, this is subtext for her own problems in life that, in turn, form part of the story's drive. Later, when Jules becomes dangerously comfortable in this new world and has a sexual affair with Paul, she realises that it can't last, and that only when she can unite the two worlds – what she's learnt from Paul's world and what she loves about Nic and her family's world – will she be happy. She does return, of course, and there's a sense that the old world is now different. It's been allowed to grow, and will be harmonious once more.

Barbara's world in *Notes on a Scandal* (scr. Patrick Marber, 2006) is set up as poisonous, deceitful and desperate from the word go. Her voiceover narration clearly depicts her attitude towards the school she works at, and the pupils and staff in it – very bleak. She stands, looking almost like an old crone, peering out of a window at the playground and telling us of the not-so-delightful things she foresees this term – thuggish behaviour and pupils who don't want to learn. In her class, she commands the pupils with an acid stare, and, in the background, we hear someone call her 'poison grandmother'. She watches from the wings as her colleagues flock around new teacher, Sheba Hart, finding pleasure in them making fools of themselves. In the first meeting of the term, the headmaster congratulates everyone for getting their departmental reports in – but wonders why Barbara's report is only a page long. She replies that she spent all summer writing it. Clearly, not only is she not very well liked by her colleagues, she's not understood – who is this woman? They know her in the public world, but what's her private world like?

Barbara's private world is solitary and lonely, and, as we learn, the only reality is her diary. Key to the narrative of this film is Barbara's desire to protect her world – to keep it for herself, apart from those she invites into it. This is depicted nicely when, at Christmas, Barbara's sister-in-law comes into the room that she's sleeping in. Barbara doesn't want her in there – she doesn't want anyone knowing her business – but her cat provides an opportunity for infiltration when her sister-in-law goes over to stroke it. Barbara is very uncomfortable with this event, feeling that her world has been betrayed by the entrance of someone absolutely uninvited. In a similar scene elsewhere in the film, colleague Brian comes to see Barbara, inviting himself into her flat. She's suspicious at first – what does this man want? – but it soon becomes clear that he fancies Sheba and wants to ask Barbara for advice about wooing her. Jealous and desperate, Barbara lets slip that Sheba's been having a sexual affair with one of their pupils. But it's all done in the subtlest of ways, of course.

What's special about this film is how Barbara's world dominates everything – how she slowly but surely pushes Sheba out of her seemingly happy world and lures her into her own dark, murky world. Before she's able to pounce, Barbara's given an insight into Sheba's world. It's a world characterised by family, fun and frivolity, which Barbara feels really uncomfortable in. We see her painfully trying to step into Sheba's bohemian world, but it's no good – Barbara must steal Sheba from this life and keep her for herself. So, when the opportunity comes up, she uses her malicious powers to make Sheba think she has no alternative but to leave her own world and enter Barbara's. Little does she know how it's been planned all along. Only when Sheba stumbles on little gold stars – the ones she uses in her diary when it's been a 'good' day – does the truth unravel. The gold star is an important object in providing a crack in Barbara's world that Sheba is then able to prise open. The trail of stars leads to Sheba finding Barbara's diary, and all hell breaking lose. Barbara's world is destroyed – physically (Sheba wrecks the flat) as well as metaphorically (their friendship will never be the same again) – until, at the very end, she finds another potential victim.

Drop Dead Gorgeous (scr. Lona Williams, 1999), for the majority of the film, offers us two distinct worlds – Amber's world and Gladys and Rebecca's world. Amber lives in a trailer park in the not-so-nice part of town, with her alcoholic – and later disabled – mother. She works two part-time jobs, one cleaning food trays at the local college, and one 'dressing up' dead bodies at the local funeral home. Her physical world is far from glamorous, but her inner world – Amber's personality and attitude – is calm, controlled and pretty idealistic. She never says a bad word about anyone, and just wants to have a good, 'normal' life. This is starkly contrasted with the world of Gladys and Rebecca Leeman – a sinister world of greed, deception, and, as we later learn, murder. Apart from the obvious contrasts in their inner worlds – Gladys and Rebecca are, quite frankly, evil – their physical world is also very different to Amber's. Their family home is a mansion, which we're introduced to rather melodramatically in an advertisement-style segment; their dress is stylish, almost pretentious; their hobbies are ostensibly bourgeois; even their world views are narrow-minded and, although they don't realise it, very prejudiced. The clash of these two worlds provides the central conflict for the film – Gladys and Rebecca's determination to stop Amber (and others) from being crowned Miss Mount Rose.

Towards the end of the film, we're then introduced to another world – that of Sarah Rose Cosmetics, the company sponsoring the beauty pageant. Although we've seen fragments of this world before through its effect on other people – last year's winner now in the bulimia wing of a hospital and an earlier year's winner now working in a slaughterhouse – we now see it for what it really is: chaotic and fraudulent. The mass vomiting in the hotel at the state-level competition, brought on by dodgy seafood, and then the company's headquarters being seized and thus the national competition being cancelled, reveal a world that none of the contestants has been expecting. As well as providing obvious humour, this third world makes it glaringly obvious that Amber deserves better, and could never operate truly in that world. So much so, in fact, that when the newscaster is shot by Gladys, who has escaped from the prison in which she has been recently incarcerated, Amber 'saves the day' by taking over the newscast – and is so impressive that she's hired by the broadcaster and becomes the journalist that she always wanted to be, in a world that's much more safe and fitting.

Juno (scr. Diablo Cody, 2007) starts by showing us the world of Juno MacGuff, a down-to-earth world of family, friends, bacon bits, barfing, wisecracking shopkeepers and – crucially – teenage pregnancy. In fact, it's Juno herself who guides us through this world through point of view (she's our protagonist) and commentary (her humorous voiceover). When she gets pregnant and decides to give the baby up for adoption, she, and we, are taken into a whole new world – that of Vanessa and Mark Loring. Juno has chosen the Lorings to be her baby's adoptive parents. And as soon as we meet the Lorings, we know we're in a totally different world – a world that, we guess, is going to change Juno in some way, and also a world that Juno herself may change. Visually, the two worlds couldn't be more different. Juno comes from a neighbourhood where the houses are small, close together and have a definite 'lived in' look. Vanessa and Mark live in a pristine world where the houses are big, spaced out and look more like show homes than places where people actually live. On her first visit, Juno explores the house, sneaking into the bathroom and trying out Vanessa's creams and perfumes. This is something she's not used to. As we see, her stepmother is more interested in collecting pictures and ornaments of dogs.

These two worlds are differentiated by dialogue, too – the voice of the worlds. Just from what we hear – the topics of conversation – we get a real sense of what these worlds are about. For example, Juno's world is characterised by pee sticks, Sunny D, pregnancy as a problem, teenage abortion, sex, pork swords, menstruation, condoms, balls, a garbage dump of a situation, blood and guts, sea monkeys, Taco Bell, tanning beds and t-shirt guns. In stark contract, the Lorings' world is characterised by talk of pregnancy as beauty, vitamin water, legal terminology, ginseng coolers, custard and cheesecake yellow paint, reading books about childbirth, and the processes of bringing up a child. Through dialogue, then, not just visual depictions, we feel how the worlds work. We know exactly what they're about by listening to what their characters say and discuss.

What's really interesting about the two worlds of *Juno* is the transition that Mark makes between them, aided – albeit unintentionally – by Juno. From the start, we learn that Mark's not allowed to have his possessions – guitars, DVD collection, etc – on show. Vanessa's made him put them all together in one room. Mark's passion is to be a real musician, not the corporate-driven composer that he's let himself be, scoring television commercials, for example. When he tells Juno that the score for a men's razor commercial was composed by him – importantly, Juno knows this commercial well – and that it paid for the kitchen they're standing in, we get the sense that he's not happy about it. It's a means to an end. As we later learn, he wants to be a rock star. He wants to play music that he enjoys, not that merely pays the bills. When Juno jokes how she's just carrying the baby for them, and will 'squeeze it out' soon enough – a line that shocks Vanessa – Mark replies with, 'Keep it in the oven!' This is a really important line to signal the uncomfortable space that Mark inhabits – torn between the world of Vanessa and the world of Juno. As soon as he's said it, he gives a look of embarrassment. Vanessa, naturally, is also uncomfortable with it. But, dramatically, the audience picks up that this is a guy who doesn't know who he is – or who's lost the sense of who he is – and that, for him, the two worlds are going to collide. As he says to Juno, 'Here's to dovetailing interests.'

5. SHAPING CHARACTERS

It's through characters that we experience films. A screenplay is made up of lots of elements – as you'll see throughout this book – but it's through character that we really understand a story. It's through character that we see everything else – the world, action, dialogue, theme. Unless you're going to write an experimental film with no characters – good luck! – you'll have to spend a long time developing your characters. Before you start writing the screenplay, you need to plan who your characters are going to be, and what journeys they're going to undertake. As you write the screenplay, you need to think about their reactions to the situations that will bring them to life – verbally as well as through action. As you re-write and re-write some more, you're going to be constantly honing your characters – refining their physical journey, clarifying their emotional journey, shaping their relationships to others, finding their true voice, etc. There's no one way of doing this, as you'll find out from this book, but it has to be done somehow.

Films with weak characters are films that don't work. Sometimes the protagonist's backstory hasn't been explored fully, resulting in a plot that fails to connect with an audience, because there's nothing of interest to them and nothing at stake that they care about. This was the case with *Wimbledon* (scr. Adam Brooks, Jennifer Flackett & Mark Levin, 2004) – a vacuous film that pretended it was about something by slipping in a forced element of Peter's backstory at the end, rather than letting it drive the whole story. Sometimes it's hard to work out who the protagonist and antagonist are, and therefore how you're supposed to be reading the story. This was the case with *The Family Stone* (scr. Thomas Bezucha, 2005) – a sloppy film that kept shifting our allegiance between characters Meredith and Sybil, never making it clear who we were supposed to care about, and ending in a sentimental death scene (Sybil's) that had little power because we'd been constantly in flux between caring for and despising her. And sometimes the cast of characters hasn't been considered properly, resulting in too many characters to care about – such as *Love Actually* (scr. Richard Curtis, 2003) – or not enough characters to challenge and encourage the protagonist, leaving the audience with the feeling that they haven't really deserved to succeed – such as *Coco Before Chanel* (*Coco Avant Chanel*) (scr. Anne Fontaine & Camille Fontaine, 2009).

Most films guide us through the story by way of the protagonist's point of view, but some films actually use this as their selling point. The point of view being followed might be surprising or refreshing – perhaps even challenging – and truly engage an audience. *Monster* (scr. Patty Jenkins, 2003) was fascinating because it was told through the eyes of a serial killer – a real-life one at that. The framing of the film – hooking us right from the start with empathetic voiceover – helped this to work. *We Need to Talk About Kevin* (scr. Lynne Ramsay & Rory Kinnear, 2011) told us a tragic story about a mass murderer – through the eyes of his mother, Eva. It would've been easy to tell this story through the eyes of the police, or one of the victim's family members – but in choosing the murderer's mother, we saw that she, too, was a victim of his crimes, and trying to work out whether in fact she's to blame for his actions. *Shutter Island* (scr. Dennis Lehane, 2010) plays with our perceptions of truth by making us doubt the accuracy of the protagonist's story. During the middle of the film, we start to question Teddy's voice as we're given a different point of view of what's going on – that he's clinically mad, and we can't believe a word he says. With this comes a shift in the drive of the story – from Teddy solving a missing-person mystery to him trying to work out the mystery of his own life. Adaptations often work on the premise of the story being told through a different point of view, too. The challenge with any adaptation is how to make it fresh and interesting to an audience who might be really familiar with one of the existing versions – and so choosing a different character to tell the story can be effective.

Two useful books to consult for further – and deeper – work on character are Rib Davis's *Developing Characters for Script Writing* (2004) and Linda Seger's *Creating Unforgettable Characters* (1998). Both books examine character from a range of angles, from essential core to building a backstory to visualising their dramatic problem.

INNER CHARACTER

True character is closely tied to structure – it's actually really difficult to think about a screenplay's plot without thinking about the essence of character. Characters drive a screenplay, therefore they drive the action. The action itself is performed by characters, resulting in reactions to that action, and subsequently a decision about further action. In most screenplays, the true action will begin as a result of the inciting incident – a decision to act upon the challenge posed (see Chapter 6 for more on this). Therefore, all of the action undertaken by the screenplay's protagonist is a result of what we might call the **defining problem** – the specific thing that sets them on their journey, and triggers them to react.

With this, of course, comes the idea of inner character – or emotion, or core drive, or need. The action wouldn't take place – starting with the reaction to the inciting incident – if it weren't for a decision within the character to react in a certain way. The problem might be posed physically, or as a physical endeavour, and the reaction to this is physical action – but, clearly, it's been driven by something within.

This is where we explore the notion of inner character, and what it is that's driving your character to succeed. In other words, why are they doing this? What does it mean to them? The result of this on the audience – why they should care – then relates to theme. The character's story is telling them something that they can relate to – an attitude or point of view about something.

Simply, your character does as they are – or, they are what they do. If he's desperate to prove himself to his father, then his actions – regardless of the situation presented to him – are in some way going to be related to this dramatic need. If she's hell bent on revenge, then her character's bound to be coloured by that – her actions will be influenced by what's driving her, even if the situation isn't directly related to what she wants to avenge.

When developing your characters – certainly your protagonist, but also other main and secondary characters – you might want to ask **power questions** of them. Questions that will help you understand the core of your character. They're called power questions because they're what power your character – the electrical charge that drives them through their story. Useful power questions include:

- What do they want?
- What do they need?
- What do they dream of?
- What do they fear?
- What's their main strength?
- What's their main weakness?
- What's their main problem?

Such questions help you find the best dramatic and thematic tension in your characters – giving you 'high stakes' that can amplify the drama and help to shape the story. They will help you, through the development process, to find the spine of your story – the Central Dramatic Question (CDQ) and the Central Thematic Question (CTQ).

Creative exercise

Choose a film and work out what's driving the protagonist, physically and emotionally, and how that gives shape to the narrative. You might want to use the power questions above as a starting point. When you've done this, ask the same of a screenplay you're working on. What's it about, and how is it being driven by character? If you're in the early stages of development, what might you need to do to dig deeper into your character? If you're at a later stage, how might you need to express the inner life of your character more in the screenplay?

BACKSTORY

A core element of understanding inner character is backstory. In other words, where's your character come from? What's happened to them in the past that's affecting who – and how – they are now? Sometimes a character's backstory is clear to both them and us – and it has obvious effects on the plot. Other times, the character's backstory slowly emerges throughout a story – to them and to us – creating dramatic tension and sometimes a twist. As a culture, we love to know who people are, and what's happened to them in the past. It helps us to understand them 'in the now' – and our position in relation to them. That's why we love films so much.

Asking **backstory questions** – which may overlap with power questions – is a great way of learning about your characters. But you have to be careful what you ask them. It has to be revealing and relevant. For example, questions about their performance at school, how many sisters they have, what their hobbies are and how they like their eggs barely scratch the surface. They might be useful – in a screenplay about a super-intelligent only child who eats scrambled eggs so he can win every badminton match he plays, for example – but generally they're pretty banal and useless. I'm quite sceptical when I see character question lists like this. I wonder what they will actually achieve – at least in the early stages of development, when you're trying to get to the core of your character.

Instead, it's more effective to focus your questions to try and reveal something that will fuel both plot and theme. Hopes, fears, weaknesses, problems and dreams are great places to start – and you might make them more precise as you go on, digging deeper by relating core values to elements specific to your story (character, world, plot, etc). Sometimes you might need to go back and ask questions again, or ask different questions. You might get stuck on a plot point and want to find out more about your character so you can create an event or action that feels true to the story. In this way, asking questions about characters – creating their backstory – is a continuous process, all the while helping you to experiment, refresh, refine and align.

Creative exercise

Choose three characters from one or more screenplays that you're working on, and create a list of fifteen backstory questions for each character. Ask the questions and write down the answers – then evaluate how useful they've been for your work.

OUTER CHARACTER

If character is the true core of your protagonist and supporting cast, then characterisation's the way you present this on the screen – and on the page. It's about bringing characters to life – visualising and verbalising who they are and what they're concerned with. If inner character is about introspection, outer character is about execution.

Because screenwriting's a visual medium, you need to think first and foremost about how you show your audience who your characters are. It's about deploying action and other visual traits – such as appearance and surroundings – to show us who these people are and why we should care. Here are some questions you might want to consider:

- How does a character behave in a situation alien to them? Show us their reactions.

- What would a character do if they had to take all their clothes off? How does their reaction tell us more about their inner character?

- How would a kind and modest character react to a group of people who think they're superior to everyone? What would their reactions tell us about their morals?

- How would an arrogant and inconsiderate character react to people who think they're superior to everyone? What would their reaction tell us about their backstory?

- What does a character wear – and not wear? How does this symbolise their personality?

- How does a character compose themself, and is it the same in all situations? What does this tell us about their strengths and weaknesses?

- What is a character's house like? What does this tell us about their abilities?

- What kind of car does a character drive? What does this signify about their dreams?

- Where does a character spend their evenings? How might this tell us about their fears?

Constructing character is also about giving them a voice. I'll say more on writing character dialogue in Chapter 11, but for now it's necessary to hammer home the point that screen characters are also what they say – and don't say. How someone speaks, what someone speaks about, and when a character doesn't speak is all part of building a great character. Well-developed, engaging character voice is something I see missing from a lot of screenplays. So here are some things you might want to consider:

- What pattern of speech does a character use? Clear and eloquent, or quick and incoherent?What does this tell us about them?

- How does a character speak when with someone of a higher social status? What does this tell us about their hopes?

- How does a character speak when with someone younger and less experienced? What does this tell us about their fears?

- What kind of vocabulary does a character use? How does this illuminate their personality?

- What cultural, political or religious references does a character use? What does this tell us about their upbringing?

- When is a character purposely being silent? What does this tell us about their feelings?

A great example of character voice is Barbara's in *Notes on a Scandal*. Her voice – vocabulary, pace, tone, topic – is infectious. As well as making it crystal clear who she is, it characterises the world – her world – and how we're supposed to feel about it. She's an extremely quick thinker and very articulate, using words to pull Sheba, and us, into her world and manipulate her until she's destroyed. Her voiceover – acerbic, musical, damaging – lures us into the story, making us want to know how and why she's become like this.

PROTAGONISM AND ANTAGONISM

There's a special relationship between the protagonist and antagonist. At one end of the spectrum, they couldn't be more different – they're at odds with one other throughout the screenplay, symbolising the extremes of good and bad – of pure and evil. They provide much of the conflict in a story as they try to out-do each other and, in some cases, kill or physically damage one another. They often want the same thing – or a version of the same thing – and so will do anything to get their reward. At the other end of the spectrum, they're actually quite similar. They want the same thing – though for different reasons – and so share some ideas and qualities. Also, they need each other. The protagonist wouldn't be so without the antagonist – not just in terms of us working out the opposing roles, but the protagonist wouldn't become a 'hero' if it weren't for the antagonist laying down traps and obstacles – or worse. And vice versa. In this way, then, they're almost like two sides of the same coin and, although they spend most of the time in battle, they're intrinsically connected.

Sometimes, the protagonist and antagonist are the same person – or at least different parts of the same person, such as a memory or a projection. This is the case with *Fight Club* (scr. Jim Uhls, 1999) and *Me, Myself and Irene* (scr. Peter Farrelly, Mike Cerrone & Bobby Farrelly, 2000).

When developing a screenplay, it's crucial that you find the right kind of antagonist for your protagonist and story. Antagonists aren't one-size-fits-all – they should be explored and crafted to provide the right type and amount of antagonism to bring out the emotional journey of your protagonist. Not only that, they should be relevant to the story world, genre and theme. Primary antagonism doesn't always come in the form of another character – it might be the environment, a rule in the world, or the self, for example – but it's always relevant to the protagonist's emotional journey. Anyone can throw down physical obstacles and make threats, but not everyone can do or say something that directly affects the protagonist's inner character – something that hits a raw nerve and propels them to succeed.

Creative exercise

For each of the following story situations, find five protagonists and five antagonists. Consider how they'd work as a dramatic pairing – what repels them from one another, and what attracts them? Also, how do they work specifically for the situation that's been set?

- A sci-fi about a group of first-time space explorers sent to a newly discovered planet
- A romantic comedy set in a nursing home by the seaside
- A sports film about a group of disabled hockey players
- A political thriller set around the threat of a global oil strike
- A children's adventure about a group of school children who go on a summer camp

---

CAST DESIGN

It's not only individual characters that are important to a screenplay, but the relationships they're in. A character on their own can only show us so much – a character in relation to others can give us much more information about emotions, attitudes, values, power, hopes and fears. Although a character is almost always consistent, they can show different sides when they're with other people. This lets the audience see for themselves the complexity and depth of the story, without having to spell it out in expositional ways.

This is where cast design comes in. Essentially, it's about finding the right set of characters to tell your story – the right cast to explore the world and its themes. These relationships between characters are important both dramatically and thematically. Depicting both conflict and camaraderie, they force characters to show what they want, challenge them in their emotional arc, and make them act and react to events going on around them. When crafted well, these relationships can also vibrate with deeper thematic meaning, reflecting the central character journey or theme. With good cast design, then, you can tell your audience about many aspects of the world we live in, about your values as a writer, and, by exploring such relationships, echo your audience's own hopes, fears, successes and failures.

When designing a cast for your screenplay, you might want to think about the following:

- Who needs to be in your story world? Who does your protagonist need to be in conflict and camaraderie with, in order to undergo an emotional arc?

- How many are key players in your screenplay, and how many secondary? What are their relationships to one another – who likes whom and who hates whom, etc?

- Considering them as a dramatic whole, what's this cast about? How are they connected (family, place, theme, job, etc) and how are they disconnected?

- What makes your cast distinctive? How's it balanced with an array of characters – defined by age, appearance, status, role, personality, etc?

- What binds your cast together in hard times? As a dramatic whole, is there something they all represent?

A really useful book to look at here is William Indick's *Psychology for Screenwriters* (2004). In the book, Indick applies the work of various psychological theorists to screenwriting. Two of these theorists, Carl Jung and Rollo May, are concerned with character archetypes, which is really useful for understanding character functions. Indick gives plenty of examples of these archetypes in action, so you should be able to understand how the ideas work in practice. And, because these works help us to understand character functions – as opposed to character execution – we start to understand the roles that characters take in a screenplay, both individually and collectively. We learn that, in some way, all the characters in a screenplay reflect aspects of the protagonist, and that the protagonist needs to integrate the qualities from these characters to succeed on their journey. And so, looking at work like this helps us to better understand cast design – to understand the dynamics required of a group of characters used to tell a story. As such, as well as adding flavour and texture to a screenplay, good cast design ensures that the audience will remain interested in, and connected to, the story.

The Kids Are All Right is a good illustration of well-crafted and interesting cast design, resulting in dynamic character relationships. Mother Nic and daughter Joni (who she gave birth to) are very similar – academic, ambitious, somewhat sheltered. Second mother Jules and son Laser (who she gave birth to) are very similar – not so academic, doers, enjoying life. Sperm-donor father Paul is more like Jules and Laser, though he is successful as well, with his own thriving business. When all of these characters are put together, some really interesting and complex transformations take place. Nic, for example, becomes even more extreme in her control of the family, before eventually relaxing and connecting with Paul. Jules becomes even more frivolous by embarking on a sexual affair with Paul, though, when he confesses that he's falling for her, she retracts and misses all the things she has with Nic. Interestingly, it's through the same scene that we see these reversals. Nic finally 'lets go' and enjoys Paul's company, complimenting him on his cooking and singing a Joni Mitchell song with him. Jules, however, is now fearful of the secret coming out, and seeing Nic and Paul getting along makes her uncomfortable and paranoid. It's when Nic goes to the bathroom and finds Jules' hair that the story takes on a different shift – the secret out. Playing out underneath all this is Joni's character arc. She's academic, focused and prudish but, learning about the harsh realities of life through the revelation of Jules and Paul's affair, she drops her guard, gets drunk and eventually kisses 'good boy' Jai. She soon regrets this, but has at least learnt about herself, life and other people. What's interesting here is that it's her friend Sasha who's been encouraging her to 'get it on' with Jai from the very start. There are clear parallels here between their relationship and Nic and Jules' relationship, which provides great dramatic texture and, through parallel character pairings, reinforces the themes of identity, experimentation and being true to oneself. Laser's arc, albeit on a smaller scale, is also important in this web of character relationships. Through Paul – who advises and shows him a way of being true to yourself – he ditches his controlling, sometimes aggressive friend Clay, knowing that he's not the kind of guy he wants to be around. Again, there's a really interesting parallel here with Nic and Jules, who also share some of these traits and problems.

In the film *In America* (scr. Jim Sheridan, Naomi Sheridan & Kirsten Sheridan, 2002), Christy functions as Johnny's mentor as well as being his daughter – which again offers us an interesting set of character dynamics. Christy feels like she's the one propping the family up, as she tells Johnny towards the end of the film. She's also the one who forces Johnny to 'say goodbye to Frankie' at the end of the film, which has been his inherent problem throughout the story. Thus, although she's his daughter, and he should be the one looking after her, she's the one who actually makes his character arc happen, leading him to accept his son's death. She's then able to leave him in the comfort of his wife Sarah – where he should have been all along, but whose relationship has been fractured since the death of their son. A key scene in the film to show this rich character dynamic – daughter looking after father, and willing him to move on – comes when Christy sings the song *Desperado* at a school concert. The words to this song are a clear hint at what Johnny needs to do – she's pleading with him. As she sings, Johnny films her on the camcorder, zooming in to her face. This makes the meaning of the song very personal – that he needs to listen to what she's saying. She can't keep going on like this – she needs her father to move on and be a father again. As she says to Johnny later in the film, when they're both almost at breaking point, she's a child – and she cried, too.

> **Creative exercise**
> Think about your own life, and how you might dramatise it – or parts of it – as a film. With you as the protagonist, who would you need around you to help tell your story? Which people would become characters in your screenplay, and which people would you not need? What would your chosen characters' functions be? How would they work to tell the story of your life?

MINOR CHARACTERS

Aside from main and secondary characters, minor characters can also add flavour and texture to a screenplay. More characters means a bigger budget, of course, but sometimes that can be worth it because of the added dimension that they bring. I once worked on a feature film where, through the script-editing process, we added in minor characters to help build the comedy value of the screenplay – characters who appeared in backgrounds, sometimes just passing, and sometimes uttering a couple of words or giving a look. Unfortunately, most of these had to be stripped out again once the film was made – because they cost too much. I think the film suffered because of this, but it was just the reality of the situation. Ideally, budgets would be limitless – or actors would be free – and minor characters would be able to be used much more to give that extra flavour and texture that some screenplays need.

Minor characters aren't just there for the sake of it, either. They add to the fabric of the story by fulfilling one (or more) of four functions –

to instigate, illuminate, imitate or innovate. A minor character might **instigate** action and/or emotion, play a literal part in shaping the plot and/or the character arc. They're someone who moves the story on, shifting or diverting narrative emphasis, or someone who pushes or pulls the protagonist on their journey. They might only appear for one scene, but their function is to manipulate the plot for a specific dramatic purpose – a spoke in the wheel. Blake in *Glengarry Glen Ross* (scr. David Mamet, 1992) only appears for one scene, but directs the whole story for all the characters – he is the inciting incident. Minor characters might also be an obstacle for the protagonist to overcome – the gatekeeper, the henchman, the possessor of vital information, etc.

Minor characters can also **illuminate** the protagonist or other main characters. Seeing what a minor character is or isn't helps to define the more important characters. This can be demonstrated through roles – who one is in comparison to the other. Personality is another thing minor characters can help to illuminate – how they act and how they look can work as a stark contrast to the protagonist. Seeing and understanding the minor character helps us to see and understand the protagonist, for example. What others say and feel about the protagonist or other main characters is another way of illumination. Minor characters can come in useful here, giving us the information we need to get a better sense of the more important characters.

Minor characters can also be used to **imitate** or mirror what's going on thematically in the screenplay. In *Lost in Translation* (scr. Sophia Coppola, 2003), for example, the prostitute who comes to Bob's room, play-acting to try and arouse him, the youths in the games arcade, interacting with virtual reality, and Kelly, the so-called actress, who checks into the hotel using a pseudonym and lives her life through surface images, are all minor characters who reflect the film's theme of dislocation and loss of reality. They're minor characters, but through them the screenplay's portrayal of theme is enriched – making it more engaging for the audience. Minor characters might also be used as symbols to represent the film's genre, or at least visually remind the audience that they're watching – and should be feeling – a particular type of story. These might come in the form of background characters, again adding flavour and texture to the film.

Finally, minor characters can be used to **innovate** a screenplay – to make the writing come alive and give the film a distinctive feel. This can also make the screenplay feel authored, the writer's voice all over it – their own authentic style. If screenwriters tell stories with universal concerns at their heart, then using minor characters can be a way to make the execution unique. Minor characters add colour – like a palette of paints – giving the screenplay an entertaining and refreshing feel. Well defined and diverse, they don't just appeal to the audience, either – they add visual and aural pace to the screenplay, which can be important for someone reading it.

The use of minor characters in *Drop Dead Gorgeous* gives the film a really rich texture that fits its mockumentary style – a parody of the documentary, with its focus on the goings-on of 'everyday' life, and, as such, life's varied and peculiar characters. And so we have Chloris, the over-weighty, chain-smoking choreographer; judge John, the pervert who desperately tries to cover his liking for young girls; judge Jean, the drab-looking employee of Lester Leeman, who never actually utters a word throughout the film, only frowns; judges Harold and Hank, social misfits who constantly fight in front of the cameras; and Amber's mother's friend Loretta, quick-witted and sexually minded. These characters, and many more, combine to create a rich, dynamic and hilarious cast that complements the ridiculous – but fascinating – world of the Mount Rose beauty pageant.

6. DESIGNING A STRUCTURE

Like it or loathe it, structure is really important in screenwriting. Not only is it an integral part of telling your story, it's an integral part of telling others about your story. Those reading or commissioning screenplays want to know what happens – and so you need to let them know how your story's going to be told. They want to know why it happens, too – the themes you're trying to convey – but it's no exaggeration to say that those in the industry are driven to know how exactly this film's going to be played out. They want to see the action themselves so they can imagine an audience watching – and hopefully enjoying – it.

Although some screenwriters have a bad relationship with structure, good screenwriters know how to use it well. They're not bound by it, nor are they afraid of it. Instead, they use it to get to the heart of their story, and then freely play with it when their gut tells them it's not working properly. It's easy to see why some of the structural terminology used in screenwriting – inciting incident, act turning point, midpoint, climax, etc – can be off-putting and seem formulaic. But when you think about it, it's only a way of expressing what we already know and do anyway. We all experience moments where something big happens that calls into question our actions, views or beliefs – the inciting incident. And we all experience times when we suddenly find ourselves doubting our actions, and reconsider what we're doing – the midpoint. Our characters experience these, too. And so giving these moments a name isn't about enforcing rules or rigidity – it's about creating a language that we can all understand and enjoy.

CHARACTER JOURNEYS

The word **journey** is used a lot in screenwriting. It's a way of expressing the arc that the character undergoes, emotionally as well as physically. And because a screenplay's a progression of time – characters advancing in the narrative, even if the narrative's told in non-chronological order – we use the word journey to capture the idea of characters moving forward, undertaking action and learning things about themselves and the world as a result. Some films have obvious journeys, like adventure stories and road movies. Think of *Big Fish* (scr. John August, 2003) and *The Adventures of Priscilla, Queen of the Desert* (scr. Stephan Elliott, 1994), for example. But other films have more subtle journeys, such as redemption plots and personal dramas. Think of *The Lives of Others* (scr. Florian Henckel von Donnersmarck, 2006) and *Girl, Interrupted* (scr. James Mangold, Lisa Loomer & Anna Hamilton Phelan, 1999), for example. Whatever the genre or form, all films are about journeys – and it's that journey that connects with the audience, to ensure they keep watching.

Journeys are made up of two parts – the **physical journey** and the **emotional journey**. Like strands of DNA, they're part of the fabric of screenplay structure, continually intertwining to create the whole. It's another way of saying that a screenplay is comprised of story and plot – the **story** is what it's about, and the **plot** is how it's told, through action. You can't have one without the other, not really. A story without a plot isn't a screenplay – it's an idea. A plot without a story is directionless and meaningless – a waste of time, actually. *Prometheus* (scr. Jon Spaihts & Damon Lindelof, 2012) is a good example of this – a film that had lots of special effects, fast-paced action and even a vivid story world, but no story. What was that film really about? Whose journey was it? Apart from wondering what these paranormal entities were, why did we care about this film? There was potential to use the character of Elizabeth as an emotional guide through the story, but the screenplay was so under-developed that all we could do was write it off as a bad experience. It felt more like a set-up for a sequel than it did a film in its own right, this first instalment working as the equivalent of an Act 1 – with no emotional arc at all. Another film that fails miserably because of this type of approach is *The Golden Compass* (scr. Chris Weitz, 2007) – again, a film where nothing really happens and nobody arcs, leaving a feeling of narrative hollowness. Therefore, it's always useful to think of your screenplay as a physical representation of an emotional arc – a plot used to tell a story, one that, through the telling, releases at least one but usually a series of themes. This is what makes a good screenplay. And you want to write good screenplays, right?

Physical journeys, in essence, are about what the character wants. As an audience, we see them trying to achieve something physical. It's a tangible goal that we literally see them in pursuit of, driven by a motivation that's usually brought about by the inciting incident. Examples might include:

- Geoff has to get to Los Angeles by the end of the week, to bury his dead mother.

- Karina has to find her way out of the forest, before it gets dark.

- The cop wants to catch the killer before she strikes again.

- Alfred desperately wants Molly to agree to marry him, so he can show his workmates that he's capable of commitment.

Emotional journeys are about what happens to the character as a result of pursuing their want. As an audience, we see them undergoing an emotional arc. It's understood as what the character needs – the subconscious thing that's been driving them all along. It might be something that lurks in their past, but has been stirred up early on in the screenplay. Or it might be something that they, unlike the other characters and the audience, were totally oblivious of. Examples might include:

- Geoff finally understands the hardship his mother underwent to give him the best chance in life – and now it's too late.

- Karina learns that she shouldn't betray her parents' wishes, and that she does need their care and love after all.

- The cop realises that he's not God, and that he must learn to work in a team if he wants to succeed.

- Alfred learns the true value of love, and that he shouldn't care what others think.

Creative exercise

Choose a film and write about the relationship between the protagonist's physical and emotional journeys. What's the story at the heart of the screenplay? How has it been plotted? Where you can, identify key plot turning points that serve the protagonist's emotional arc.

THREE-ACT STRUCTURE

The most understood and widely used base for a screenplay narrative is the three-act structure. In fact, it's the base for understanding all other structural models, from Joseph Campbell's *The Hero with a Thousand Faces* (1993) to Christopher Vogler's *The Writer's Journey* (2007), and Paul Joseph Gulino's *Screenwriting: The Sequence Approach* (2004) to Linda Aronson's *The 21st-Century Screenplay: A Comprehensive Guide to Writing Tomorrow's Films* (2011). Although some are sceptical about it, seeing it as rigid and formulaic, it's actually flexible and expandable. It's so broad and sweeping that it acts more as a 'container' for a story to occur in – a frame that your unique story can be composed within. The three-act structure sees a story divided into a beginning (Act 1), a middle (Act 2) and an end (Act 3), with key turning points between the acts. Syd Field is often seen as the pioneer for the three-act structure in screenwriting – see, for example, *The Definitive Guide to Screenwriting* (2003) – but it actually goes as far back as Aristotle, who also saw that drama was composed of a beginning, middle and end, and that the circular feel to a story – coming back to the beginning again, but in a different way – was both practical and appealing. Ari Hiltunen's *Aristotle in Hollywood: The Anatomy of Successful Storytelling* (2002) is a useful book here. As the title suggests, what we see here is a practical application of Aristotle's theories to contemporary cinema.

Three-act structure, then, helps the screenwriter to start structuring their story from its basic building blocks, and can be broken down as follows:

- **Act 1, Beginning/Setup/Establishment** (¼) – introduces the protagonist and other central characters, establishes the story world, and sets up the dramatic situation of the story, and its associated themes. Through the **inciting incident**, the physical goal of the protagonist is identified – what they want to achieve or accomplish by the end of the screenplay. Act 1 also identifies what's at stake for the protagonist – what they stand to lose if the goal isn't achieved. It also sets up the main antagonistic forces (people, events, ideologies) that will pose problems (obstacles, hurdles) for the protagonist to overcome in pursuit of the goal.

- **Act 2, Middle/Confrontation/Complications** (½) – where the journey truly starts. Deciding to undertake a challenge to achieve the goal, the protagonist's physical journey begins and progresses at speed – often with an early setback, reminding them that it's not going to be easy. Obstacles are met and overcome, testing the protagonist's abilities and dedication to the challenge. Conflict is crucial in Act 2, for both the audience (excitement, engagement) and the protagonist (testing, pushing). The protagonist has new experiences and meets new friends and enemies, all of which help them grow. What's important in Act 2 – especially during and after the midpoint – is that the protagonist identifies they have emotional needs, and, when confronting them, begins to arc. Act 2 often ends on a low point, where all seems lost – physically and emotionally.

- **Act 3, End/Resolution/Re-Establishment** (¼) – where the protagonist gets or doesn't get what they want. This is a climactic moment, offering catharsis to the audience. The narrative begins to wind down or change direction, which is an important moment of reflection on all that's happened. In most films the protagonist's goal is achieved, although sometimes it's achieved in a different way than expected. Sometimes the goal isn't achieved, which can be tragic – or a blessing in disguise. The protagonist often then goes back to the beginning, to where they started, either physically or metaphorically. However, the original world's now changed – or at least their view of it – and things will never be the same again.

Here's a summary of the three-act structure, drawn from above:

The disturbance in a character's life sets them on a journey to achieve a goal, which incorporates a physical want and an emotional need. Obstacles stand in their way, creating a series of rising conflicts that need to be overcome before the goal can be achieved and resolution found.

The inciting incident

Referred to above, the inciting incident is an important moment – or series of moments – in a screenplay. Occurring during Act 1 – usually 10 or 15 minutes in – it's the key disturbance of the story that sets everything in motion. It's the moment of disequilibrium in the protagonist's world. It's their call to adventure. The inciting incident propels the protagonist on their journey, more often than not appearing in the form of a problem posed or a challenge set. **Motivation** is crucial in screenwriting, and this is where the inciting incident comes in. Essentially, if the protagonist doesn't have an impetus to undertake the challenge that's been set, then the story can lack conviction and the audience won't care if they achieve their goal or not. So, the inciting incident offers a dilemma or crisis where the protagonist must decide whether to undertake the challenge or not – for better or for worse.

The inciting incident comes in many forms, but here are some common ones:

- **Someone sets a literal challenge** – the task is to complete it by a given deadline. If there's no challenge, there's no story. In *How to Lose a Guy in 10 Days* (scr. Kristen Buckley, Brian Regan & Burr Steers, 2003), magazine feature writer Andie sets herself the challenge of finding a boyfriend and then making him dump her in 10 days. Ironically, at the very same time, advertising guy Ben is set his own challenge – to make a girl fall in love with him in 10 days. In *Invictus* (scr. Anthony Peckham, 2009), Nelson Mandela sets South Africa rugby captain François Pienaar the challenge of getting his team, the Springboks, to the Rugby World Cup Final. He tells him that this is more than just a game of sport – the future of their country depends on it.

- **Boy meets girl (or boy meets boy/girl meets girl) for the first time** – one realises they must chase the other to earn their love. If there's no meeting, there's no chase – and so no story. In *My Big Fat Greek Wedding* (scr. Nia Vardalos, 2002), Toula serves hot guy Gus in her family-run restaurant. She instantly falls in love, even though he doesn't notice her, igniting in her a commitment to change – physically and emotionally. In *Brokeback Mountain* (scr. Larry McMurtry & Diana Ossana, 2005), Jack and Ennis are put on the same watch. In their tent, cold and lonely, they share an intimate sexual experience. Their lives will never be the same again.

- **Someone sees something they really want** – the goal's to try and get it, often by whatever means possible. Nothing seen means nothing sought – and, again, no story. In *There Will Be Blood* (scr. Paul Thomas Anderson, 2007), Daniel's already begun his successful oil empire when Paul pays him a visit to tell him about the oil in Little Boston. Daniel can't resist the temptation, so sets off on a new venture to try and make even more money. In *Ratatouille*, Remy is obsessed with famous chef Auguste Gusteau – he wants to be a magnificent cook, just like him. But when Gusteau dies, in the wake of a bad review from food critic Anton Ego, his legacy is evaporating. This makes Remy even more adamant to pursue his love of food and cooking so, when he's carried away in the sewers from his family and finds himself in the middle of Paris, he decides to follow his dream of working in Gusteau's restaurant.

- **Something's stolen or taken away** – the goal's to try and recover it, often by a given deadline. If nothing's stolen, then there's no reason for anyone to try and find anything – and the deadline adds extra motivation. In *Catch Me If You Can* (scr. Jeff Nathanson, 2002), Frank's lifestyle and happiness are taken away from him. His family have to give up their house – and mum and dad file for divorce. When asked where he wants to live, he runs away, and, in an attempt to regain the lost money (and the depleted family), he embarks on a journey of con-artistry. All the while, he's being chased by FBI agent Carl. In *The Girl with the Dragon Tattoo* (scr. Nikolaj Arcel & Rasmus Heisterberg, 2009), Mikael's freedom has been taken away – he's going to prison in six months. At the same time, Henrik is desperate to find out what happened to Harriet, his niece who disappeared 40 years earlier. Henrik employs Mikael to find out the truth – before he's sent off to prison.

- **Someone dies or is injured** – triggering a goal of revenge and affirmation, or a goal of being healed. No death or injury means no impetus to seek revenge or healing – and no story. In *Kill Bill* (scr. Quentin Tarantino, 2003), 'The Bride' comes out of a coma and remembers how she got there – she was gunned down at her wedding by former lover Bill, and his assassin assailants. Realising her husband-to-be and unborn child are dead, she undertakes a dark mission fuelled by revenge. In *Bran Nue Dae* (scr. Reg Cribb, Rachel Perkins & Jimmy Chi, 2009), Willie is sick to death of being ostracised by Father Benedictus for being Aboriginal. So, in an attempt to re-build his confidence – and follow his heart and woo love interest, Rosie – he runs away from the religious school and journeys back to Broome.

Case Study

Even today, *The Wizard of Oz* (scr. Noel Langley, Florence Ryerson & Edgar Allan Woolf, 1939) remains a fantastic case study to show how structure can be used effectively to tell a great story.

Dorothy Gale is living an unhappy life on the family farm. She craves a better life, somewhere 'over the rainbow'. She feels unwanted, and that others see her as a silly girl who just gets in the way. So she decides to run away. We see clearly here Dorothy's dramatic want – to run away – and also her need – to feel wanted and useful. This plan is scuppered, though, when fake fortune teller Professor Marvel tells her she must go back home to tend to her sick and worried Aunt Em. As she gets back, though, the inciting incident literally spins the action in another direction when a storm tears Dorothy's house from the ground and blows it away. The reason that Dorothy's in the house on her own is because she missed the chance of going into the storm shelter with her family – which reinforces the journey that she'll go on to feel reconnected with her family and home.

Now 'over the rainbow', Dorothy leaves the house and finds herself in the land of Oz. Here she's faced with a world starkly different to the one she left behind – it's full of colour, strange objects, and little people called Munchkins. Clearly, Dorothy's in a new world that will give her new experiences. Glinda, the good witch, tells her that, to get back to Kansas, she must find the Wizard of Oz. But that's going to take a long journey down the yellow brick road. And so the idea is clearly set up that Dorothy's going to travel a physical journey, and that, on this journey, she'll also experience emotional transformation.

The journey is not useful, of course, unless it's got conflict and obstacles. What Dorothy doesn't know is that the house landed on and killed the Wicked Witch of the East – and now her sister, the Wicked Witch of the West, is out to get her. Even worse, Dorothy's got the magical ruby slippers the Wicked Witch desperately wants, which gives her a physical motivation, too. And so, the Wicked Witch is the antagonist who'll do whatever she can to destroy an innocent Dorothy.

The Act 1 turning point occurs when Dorothy steps onto the yellow brick road to start her journey. Encouraged by the Munchkins' song, she commits to the journey – her goal to find the Wizard of Oz. Along the long journey – Act 2 – she meets her new friends, the Scarecrow,

Tin Man and Cowardly Lion. They're instrumental in helping her along, and later help her to physically achieve her goal. Emotionally, too, they develop Dorothy's character, each representing something that Dorothy lacks and needs – a brain, a heart and courage.

Conflict is encountered along the journey, much of it initiated by the Wicked Witch – apple-throwing trees, scary woods, poisonous poppies, flying monkeys, etc. These obstacles are essential to the story because they stall the happy ending Dorothy's looking for and teach her valuable life lessons – without them, meeting the Wizard would be all too easy, and Dorothy wouldn't earn her reward.

The reward itself is stalled even further when the Wizard is revealed to be a fake. Dorothy is distressed, feeling that she'll never get home, but the Wizard sets her one final test – to kill the Wicked Witch and bring back her broom. This is the Act 2 turning point, where all seems lost and the stakes are raised.

The Wicked Witch captures Dorothy, who has to be rescued by her friends. During this time, she sees a vision of her Aunt Em, and realises she shouldn't have run away in the first place. This is Dorothy's 'lowest point', fearing that she'll die – and die alone. Regretting leaving Kansas, we sense her emotional arc – to value her family and be happy in Kansas. Dorothy is finally saved, but the chase isn't over yet. The Wicked Witch throws a fireball to kill Dorothy and her friends, which sets the Scarecrow alight. Dorothy quickly throws water over him to put out the fire. Unbeknownst to her, however, the Wicked Witch cannot touch water – and so melts. This is a key moment in the story because Dorothy hasn't purposely killed the witch – she's inadvertently killed her through trying to save her friend. This shows Dorothy's emotional growth – thinking of others first – and is the true turning point of her character development.

Dorothy returns to the Wizard, who promises to get her home by balloon. She says goodbye to her friends, who remind her what she's done for them. The balloon's about to go up when her dog, Toto, climbs out, and, as she retrieves him, the balloon sails off. Dorothy's really upset, but Glinda comes back and tells her that she's been able to go home all along – she just didn't realise it. She tells her to click her heels together and repeat the line, 'There's no place like home', and she'll get there – and she does.

Dorothy wakes up from this 'dream' to find herself back in Kansas. She relays the story to her family, who just laugh. She looks at them and tells them she loves them, and that she'll never run away again – after all, 'There's no place like home.' And so, as the story ends, we see that Dorothy's undertaken a journey that's not only developed her physically, but emotionally. She's arced – from unhappy girl who wants to run away, to happy, more mature girl who's learnt the value of family and home.

Tentpoles

A simple but effective way to find the key beats of your story is by identifying its tentpoles. In other words, the key turning points that will prop your story up. It's moments like these that screenplay readers are often looking for – the big action, the dramatic twists – so, although you'll develop a much more detailed overview of your story, it's good for you to know the tentpole moments early on. After all, not only will they drive and direct the story – before and after each tentpole – they give you something to aim towards if you're crafting the screenplay in sections.

The eight tentpoles of a screenplay are:

- Status Quo
- Inciting Incident / Catalyst
- End of Act 1 Turning Point
- Act 2 Midpoint
- End of Act 2 Turning Point
- Hardest Choice
- Climax / Final Battle
- Resolution and End

If you want to use these tentpoles to help develop your story, you should summarise each one in no more than a sentence or two. You can refer back to them again and again, to remind yourself of what it is you're trying to achieve. Or, to use the tent analogy once more, to help you stop your story from collapsing.

Here are two examples of the tent poles in action:

There's Something About Mary (scr. Ed Decter, John J Strauss, Peter Farrelly & Bobby Farrelly, 1998)

- Status Quo – Ted's not been able to love anyone since Mary. He's deeply miserable and needs help.

- Inciting Incident / Catalyst – Ted's friend Dom suggests he uses private detective Pat Healy to find out what Mary's like now (which fulfils his own psychopathic need to find her).

- End of Act 1 Turning Point – whilst investigating, Pat falls for Mary and, because he wants her for himself, puts Ted off by trying to make her seem ludicrously unattractive. Ted still wants her (proving that he's a good guy), and when old friend Bob tells him she's still single – and a 'fox' – he decides to go to Miami to find her.

- Act 2 Midpoint – the first half of Act 2 consists mainly of Pat trying to woo Mary, and the audience discovering what kind of man Mary wants and needs. Ted has an eventful journey to Miami and is almost tried for murder, which buys Healy time before Ted arrives (the midpoint).

- End of Act 2 Turning Point – Ted and Mary rekindle their relationship, much to the horror of Pat and Tucker. They become really close until Mary receives an anonymous letter telling her the truth about Ted, making him seem yet another stalker. She rejects him – and so it seems impossible for Mary and Ted to be together.

- Hardest Choice – realising that Mary and Brett's potential marriage was sabotaged by Tucker, Ted decides to reunite them, giving up any possibility of having Mary for himself.

- Climax / Final Battle – the truth of Mary's crazy admirers is revealed. They all gather round, insisting she choose one, battling over her until Ted arrives with Brett, who seemingly becomes the winner.

- Resolution and End – Ted walks away, his dream in tatters. But Mary runs after him, realising he's definitely the one for her. They kiss.

Leap Year (scr. Deborah Kaplan & Harry Elfont, 2010)

- Status Quo – Anna, a super-organised, rich real-estate 'home stager', desperately wants to get married. Her fiancé, Jeremy, goes away on business to Dublin – but as it's leap year, she decides to follow him and pop the question herself.

- Inciting Incident / Catalyst – terrible weather forces Anna's plane to land in Wales. She's stranded, but determined to get to Ireland. She eventually reaches a place called Dingle, but it's at the wrong end of the country from where she needs to be.

- End of Act 1 Turning Point – after a disastrous start to her journey, offending the locals and decimating the room that she's staying in, she reluctantly accepts the help of local guy Declan. They hate each other, but she's got no choice – he's got a car and knows the way.

- Act 2 Midpoint – the first half of Act 2 sees the journey getting worse and worse. Anna's totally out of her comfort zone with Declan, and encounters obstacles such as stray cattle, thieves, falling down a muddy hill and missing the one and only train to Dublin. They're invited to a B&B, but have to pretend to be married – which includes them having to kiss in front of the owners and other guests (the midpoint).

- End of Act 2 Turning Point – seeing a different side to him, and knowing the truth about his past relationship, Anna warms to Declan. They've started to share some happy times on their journey – Anna learning to loosen up and have fun – but now the journey's come to an end and they've reached Dublin – and Jeremy.

- Hardest Choice – there's a sense that Anna's changed her mind about Jeremy, and fallen in love with Declan, but it's scuppered when Jeremy surprises her with his own proposal. Anna accepts and goes back to Boston with Jeremy, leaving Declan to go back to Dingle alone (false ending).

- Climax / Final Battle – there's something not right in Boston, and when Anna realises that Jeremy proposed just so they could get the apartment they wanted – and that he cares more about his belongings than her – she leaves the life she always wanted.

- Resolution and End – Anna goes back to Dingle and declares her love for Declan, saying that he's all she needed. She gets the proposal she always dreamed of when he asks her to marry him. She accepts and they kiss.

Sequences

Another way to approach screenplay structure, moving on from tentpoles, is to think about using sequences. This idea works on the notion that every screenplay is built up of a number of sequences

– usually eight – that each have a beginning, middle and end. You usually find two sequences in Act 1, four in Act 2, and two in Act 3 – but this isn't always the case, as you'll see below. In a way, each sequence is like a short film – with its own catalyst, complications and climax – and together they come together to form the full story. Likewise, each sequence has its own set of dramatic questions and answers, giving direction and dimensionality. We can see how sequences relate well to tentpoles, and so you should consider them in partnership.

Paul Joseph Gulino's book, *Screenwriting: The Sequence Approach*, goes into great detail about using sequences, and uses a variety of film examples to illuminate the points being made. But, for the purposes of this book, here's a short summary of how sequences work in a screenplay.

- **Sequence 1** establishes the story world and the 'normality' of the protagonist (who also has a problem). A disturbance to the normality, the **inciting incident**, raises the central dramatic question (usually related to the plot goal).

- **Sequence 2** shows the protagonist struggling with this new problem, leading to a decision to deal with it. This turning point becomes the end of Act 1.

- **Sequence 3** sees the protagonist trying to solve the problem with a 'plan of action', doing first what seems easiest. Often, more effort is needed (rising action) as the problem refuses to go away.

- **Sequence 4** shows the protagonist trying harder, often applying more serious tactics. Obstacles increase, requiring more effort. The stakes are raised. The **midpoint** usually comes here, spinning the action into a new direction (or with new focus – sometimes emotion prevails over action).

- **Sequence 5** sees the protagonist reacting to the midpoint change. He or she may be re-inspired by what's happened, leading to a new plan to achieve the goal.

- **Sequence 6** shows that, although the protagonist is working hard, he or she is still unsuccessful. This culminates in a new decision, which marks the end of Act 2. In stories with a happy ending, this is usually the 'lowest point'. In stories with a tragic ending, this is where things seem hopeful at last.

- **Sequence 7** sees the climax or 'biggest battle', incorporating the protagonist's 'hardest choice'. Often this is where the goal is achieved (or not achieved). Occasionally there's a false resolution, and sometimes there's a twist or unexpected event.

- **Sequence 8** shows the final resolution, both of action and emotion. Depending on the type of story, this might also be the climax scene – the final showdown. Sometimes there's an 'epilogue' that ties the ends of the story together once and for all.

To show the sequences in action, here's a breakdown of the film *Misery* (scr. William Goldman, 1990). Notice how each act also has its own driving question – something that the sequences in each act combine to fulfil.

Act 1 – *Will Paul get better?*

- Sequence 1 – Paul Sheldon is a writer. He finishes a new novel and celebrates in his usual way. As he leaves to go home, there's a snowstorm and he crashes the car (**inciting incident**). On the verge of death, he's saved by a mysterious figure.

- Sequence 2 – Paul wakes to find his saviour is Annie, a local nurse and his 'number one fan'. She says the phone lines are down but she'll take him to hospital as soon as the weather improves. She looks after him and he's grateful. She asks if she can read his new book, but is then horrified at the foul language he's used. She forces him to burn it. He's furious and heartbroken (end of Act 1).

Act 2 – *Will Paul get away?*

- Sequence 3 – feeling that Annie's unhinged, Paul has a new plan – to get away. He stockpiles painkillers and tries to be nice to her. But Annie also has a plan – she's read the latest *Misery* novel and forces Paul to write a new book to bring the character Misery back to life, the thing Paul least wants to do. She reveals that nobody knows he's there, and that she's lied to him. He's on his own.

- Sequence 4 – realising he's not safe, Paul tries all he can to get away. He manages to escape his room but can't get out of the locked house. He half-heartedly writes a new *Misery* but Annie's not happy – she demands a proper book. He suggests a celebratory dinner that she joyfully accepts. The climax of his plan comes to nothing – he tries to drug her with wine but she accidentally spills it (midpoint).

- Sequence 5 – Paul has to start from scratch with a new plan (same objective, different action). To keep Annie happy, he writes the *Misery* book. He also grows stronger as his body recovers. Buster, the detective, keeps investigating and Paul gets out of his room a second time, finding Annie's scrapbook. He realises she's a murderer and psychopath, which creates escalating danger. She returns and realises he's been out. Determined to keep him with her, she hobbles him. This is the **lowest point** and he seems more unlikely than ever to achieve his objective of escaping **(end of Act 2)**.

Act 3 – *Will Paul get away alive?*

- Sequence 6 – Paul no longer pretends to like Annie – they're open enemies, no more game playing. No more writing is shown, instead Buster cracks the case and comes to the house. Paul thinks he's saved but Annie sedates him and hides him in the cellar. Buster searches then leaves, but runs back in after hearing a crash. Paul calls out, and just as we think he'll be saved, Annie blasts Buster away with a shotgun. All external hope of rescue is now removed.

- Sequence 7 – Annie reveals her plans for a suicide pact **(imminent death)**. Paul persuades her to let him finish the book first. She agrees, and in a mirror scene to the beginning, he sets fire to *Misery* – the manuscript *she* treasures as opposed to the one she made him burn that *he* treasured. This unleashes the final **biggest battle** as they fight to the death. A false ending occurs where Paul thinks he's killed her – but Annie takes one last stab. He finally does kill her, with the pig ornament **(climax and plot resolution)**.

- Sequence 8 – back home **(objective achieved)**, Paul lunches with his agent. His 'real' book has been re-written and he's achieving the critical success he wanted **(emotional arc)**. This no longer seems as important, though, as Paul's been scarred by the experience. He's changed, and no longer wants the same thing **(thematic resolution)**. An 'open end' suggests danger will never quite go away as a waitress appears, she too proclaiming that she's his 'number one fan'.

Creative exercise

Write a sequence breakdown of your own, for a film that you admire.
What do you learn about how it works from doing this? Has it helped you
understand how any of your own screenplays are – or aren't – working?

ALTERNATIVE STRUCTURES

Screenwriters might want to divert from traditional three-act structures
and use more experimental, complex ways of telling a story. I say
complex, but in fact these days they're not that complex – audiences
are beginning to understand how non-linear films work and, because
more people are writing about them from a practical point of view,
screenwriters, too, are learning how to use them. There's not enough
space here to delve into the barrage of alternative structures in
use in contemporary screenwriting, so I just want to focus on two
– the multiple protagonist story and the parallel story. For a fuller
exploration of alternative structures, Linda Aronson's *The 21st-
Century Screenplay: A Comprehensive Guide to Writing Tomorrow's
Films* is pretty much a bible. It gives structure to what some people
call anti-structure, proving that alternative structures are governed by
their own principles – they're not just random.

For me, the key principle of a **multiple protagonist** story is that
the protagonists each have their own emotional arc, but by and large
share the physical journey. They belong to the same story world. And,
crucially – and this is what separates it from the parallel story – the
protagonists are brought together by the same inciting incident. They
wouldn't arc if it didn't happen. This multiple reaction to the same
event (or series of events) then allows a screenwriter to explore how
different people respond to the same catalytic event. As such, it's an
effective way of representing how we, as a culture and a society, react
differently to shared events. And, because the multiple protagonist

story is about individual character arcs, how our reactions have different emotional nuances.

A lot of people assume that, just because a film has more than one protagonist, it's a multiple protagonist story. I don't think this is true. Like I say above, what makes it a multiple story is individual reactions to the same inciting incident. This is the appeal – how one thing can trigger a range of responses in a variety of protagonists, responses that wouldn't have come about if it weren't for the inciting incident. And films like this aren't always easy to find. Multiple protagonist stories aren't as common as you might think. How many films do you know that have one catalytic event that sparks off a series of individual character arcs?

The Kids Are All Right is a good example of a multiple protagonist film. Its protagonists – Nic, Jules and Joni – are all affected by Laser and Joni contacting their birth father, Paul. These three protagonists all undergo an emotional arc – an individual emotional arc – that's brought about by Paul's arrival. Jules sleeps with Paul and realises that she's lost her identity. Nic, in temporarily losing Jules, realises that she's overbearing and partly to blame for Jules' feelings. And Joni grows up, learning that life isn't all a bed of roses. Interestingly, there's a clear suggestion at the end of the film that this is a multiple protagonist film. When Joni leaves for university, she, Nic, and Jules hug and say goodbye. Laser stands to one side, observing. He's been a central character in this film – as has Paul – but he's not fulfilled the role of a protagonist. Although he does undergo a small character arc himself, he's been more of an instigator of action for the other characters' arcs. What makes this film special, then, is how the arrival of one pivotal figure in three women's lives can function to change them all for ever. Clearly, it's this arrival – this inciting incident – that drives all of these emotional arcs. They wouldn't have happened without it.

Other examples of the multiple protagonist narrative structure include:

- *Glengarry Glen Ross*
- *The Banger Sisters* (scr. Bob Dolman, 2002)
- *Gosford Park* (scr. Julian Fellowes, 2001)
- *Before You Go* (scr. Shelagh Stephenson, 2002)
- *Calendar Girls* (scr. Juliette Towhidi & Tim Firth, 2003)
- *Little White Lies* (*Les Petits Mouchoirs*) (scr. Guillaume Canet, 2010)

Screenplays using **parallel story** structure are similar to multiple protagonist stories, but differ in that they usually aim to explore the same theme or emotion through different character perspectives, ones that don't necessarily have to be from the same story world. By seeing a series of interwoven stories, some of them even taking place in different eras, an audience is forced to connect to the narrative by considering the thematic or emotional driver. Key to a parallel story – again, the crucial difference between this and the multiple protagonist story – is that these protagonists don't react to the same inciting incident. They each experience their own catalytic event, either before they all come together if it's a parallel group story, or within their own narrative if it's a story that jumps between time frames and worlds. *The Best Exotic Marigold Hotel* (scr. Ol Parker, 2011) is a good example of the former, and *The Hours* (scr. David Hare, 2002) the latter.

For the screenwriter, it's really important to find interesting, original and complementary protagonists through whom a universal theme or emotion can be explored. As per any screenplay, the core of the story lies in theme or emotion portrayed, but, in the parallel story, its real unique texture is in its structural execution – the notion of one idea told through juxtaposing or complementary parallel characters and worlds.

The Best Exotic Marigold Hotel is an example of a parallel story film that could easily be misconceived as a multiple protagonist film. Yes, it's about a group of people who come together in a so-called luxury retirement village in India. But is it about the group or the individual characters? Although they function as a group, structurally there's nothing that the group as a whole strives towards. It'd be easy to think that the revelation of the retirement village not being what it was advertised as is the film's inciting incident – but that would mean that the rest of the film would need to be about their abilities to cope with that, which it isn't. It acts as a backdrop, and by the end of the film everyone does pull together and the retirement village is saved, but that's not what drives it. What drives the film is each character's individual goal – which is linked to individual inciting incidents that we see at the very start of the film. These include widow Evelyn's discovery that she's been left in debt, housekeeper Muriel losing her job, and high court judge Graham biting the bullet and leaving his profession. Therefore, the best way to understand this film is as a parallel story, where the multiple protagonists experience their own inciting incidents that propel them into joining the group situation – the retirement village community – but who actually follow their own individual physical journeys, albeit with help from one other.

Mysterious Skin (scr. Gregg Araki, 2004) is another film that could be seen as a multiple protagonist story, but that depends on what's deemed as the inciting incident. On the face of it, it's the sexual abuse in the past that looks like Neil and Brian's shared inciting incident. But this is problematic, not only because we don't know for sure from the start that this is the case – especially regarding Brian – but because this event doesn't drive each of the protagonists' physical journeys in the film. Rather, it's a reason that we understand more fully later. It's what we actually see in the present day that drives each of the protagonists, and so, because each has their own inciting incident, it's a parallel story. For Neil, it's his first act of prostitution, and how that triggers him to go on a dark journey of further prostitution, eventually leading him to New York. For Brian, it's seeing Avalyn in the TV show, which then leads to him piecing the past together and finding out what happened to him 'that night'.

As with all parallel films that take place in a different story world, we see various points of connection between the protagonists throughout this film, leading us to believe that they will come together at some point – and give us the meaning we've been looking for. These points of connection, feeding both our curiosity and our understanding, include: the picture of the baseball team (both boys are in it, and Brian comes into possession of it later, from the library); memories (or, in Brian's case, nightmares) of what happened with the coach; the figure of the coach himself (for Neil, idolising him, and for Brian, because he never understood what happened to him, projecting him as the figure of an alien); and, in the last third of the film, the character of Eric who, after Neil's departure for New York, becomes good friends with Brian. In fact, it is through Eric that Brian eventually comes to meet Neil, and the climactic – and final – point of connection comes when Neil reveals the truth to Brian, who then cradles himself into Neil. In this quite frankly beautiful scene, Brian needs to feel a connection to the absolute tragedy of the situation, and show to Neil that it's affected both of their lives forever.

Other examples of the parallel story narrative structure include:

- *Magnolia* (scr. Paul Thomas Anderson, 1999)
- *Babel* (scr. Guillermo Arriaga, 2006)
- *Me and You and Everyone We Know* (scr. Miranda July, 2005)
- *Love Actually* (scr. Richard Curtis, 2003)
- *Valentine's Day* (scr. Katherine Fugate, 2010)
- *New Year's Eve* (scr. Katherine Fugate, 2011)

Of course, we could argue that it doesn't matter how we classify such films. That a screenwriter should just write, and let the theorists worry about how to understand them. This isn't a bad argument at all. However, because many screenwriters learn through understanding how other people's stories work – as well as just writing and experimenting with their own material – I think it's important to offer such definitions and distinctions so that we might share knowledge and ideas for the benefit of others. And, of course, if we weren't interested in craft then books like this wouldn't exist!

The final word of advice from me is that you should only use an alternative structure for your screenplay if the story demands it. If you use it as a gimmick, it'll show. And it'll probably not work. But if your story needs a different kind of frame – whether it's related to theme or character – then you should explore using an alternative structure. Sometimes forcing yourself to expand your thinking – to experiment with structure – can open up possibilities that you'd never have thought of, giving you an engaging and refreshing screenplay. And that, of course, can only be a good thing.

INDUSTRY INSIGHT

Dr Christina Kallas is an award-winning writer-producer for film and television, and author of *Creative Screenwriting: Understanding Emotional Structure* (2010). Currently teaching at Columbia University and founder of the Writers Improv Studio in New York (www.writersimprovstudio.com), she has this to say:

Non-linear immersive storytelling
Cinema has the ability to represent multiple versions of reality simultaneously, and to challenge the frameworks of familiar ways of seeing and feeling. Why do we, then, continue to tell stories we've been told before, and in the most predictable and simplistic ways?

The hierarchical organisation reflected in classic storytelling's privileging of one character and his point of view over the rest has led to concepts such as one protagonist, one perspective, causality and linearity, which are taught and practised as if they were the Bible. In screenwriting, of course, it all goes back to Aristotle. And it's important to remember that Aristotelian 'pleasure' by no means signifies superficial entertainment in the sense of scattering attention, escapism, relaxation, temporary distraction or diversion. Quite the contrary: it expresses satisfaction on the rational as well as the emotional level. This

99

presupposes stories that challenge and interest the audience, that shake up their everyday lives – stories that broaden the spectrum of our experience since they intrinsically represent an experience themselves.

Cinematic narrative structures, which break our perception of the linear direction of time, create a world of quantum 'strangeness' where story time, story space and the audience's consciousness (mirroring the writer's consciousness) are intimately interrelated and inseparable. And there exists a higher dimension in which everything is interconnected. This is what I call emotional structure, because it goes beyond the classic one-dimensional cognitive perception. It approaches structure from the perspective of a more comprehensive perception than rational thinking, and goes beyond Aristotle's causality.

In non-linear storytelling, because there isn't one single character to follow, no main plot and no cause and effect, we as an audience are put in the centre of the action. We stop being observers and become participants. Whatever's happening, it's happening to us. We make an emotional journey, and that emotional journey – which mirrors the emotional journey of the storyteller – is the only thing that makes this a unity. A story. The story thus becomes an experience – an immersive experience.

There's an idea connected to this, which is why I think the term immersive storytelling – of which non-linearity, participation and emotion are intrinsic elements – is a happy one. This is the idea of going deeper. And it's in these depths that emotional truth lies. Surely, a writer's goal is to transfer the human experience as truthfully as humanly possible? Isn't that the reason we became writers in the first place?

© Christina Kallas, 2012

7. WRITING VISUALLY

I was taken aback recently when a group of students told me they couldn't find much from screenwriting books about writing visually. How could that be true? Screenwriting is the visual medium of creative writing. But, no, they assured me – as they ploughed through the books from the reading list, they could find hardly anything. And true enough, as I followed this up, most screenwriting books don't focus on the nature of writing visually – on visual storytelling as a skill that needs to be learnt and practised. Perhaps it's a given? Assumed? That if you're writing for the screen, of course you know how to write visually. But do you? What is visual storytelling? Is it just about telling a story through action, or is there more to it than that?

Charlie Moritz, in his book *Scriptwriting for the Screen* (2008), elaborates on the idea of visual storytelling by providing a whole chapter on the subject, as do Zara and I in *Writing for the Screen*. As these chapters concur, there's much more to writing visually than just thinking about the plot as action on the screen. In fact, that element scarcely scratches the surface. The screen is a rich space where visuality dominates. We don't have to imagine (a novel) and we don't really have to hear (a radio or theatre play) – we're seeing and understanding everything, whether that's on a macro level (big actions, key objects or motifs, etc) or a micro level (characters interacting with their environment, subtle bodily inflections, etc).

THINKING VISUALLY

Screenwriting is about visualising a story. You're writing for the screen – whatever type of screen that may be – so it's your task to think about what an audience is seeing and how that can convey meaning about story and character. Hopefully you're already interested in this. You might be someone who watches the world and tries to imagine what's going on. You might be someone who actively makes meaning of everything you see: people; places; objects; colours; materials. As a screenwriter, you should be someone who's willing to think visually and experiment with using symbolism and motif. You should love voices, but you should also love images.

It sounds like another cliché, but seeing really is believing. If a character tells you something, you might believe them. But if a character shows you something, either outright or through subtext, you're more likely to believe them. Why? Maybe it's because we trust our eyes more than our ears, and know that, if we've seen it, it's less likely to have been altered or manipulated for someone else's intention. Even better, of course, is hearing and seeing at the same time; seeing the reality of the situation through what's going on in the scene, then having this complemented – or juxtaposed, even – by someone's attempt to articulate it. And that's the power that the screen has over any other creative writing medium – the power to visualise character, visualise story, and, together, visualise emotion.

As a screenwriter, then, think of yourself as someone composing the screen. Of course it's the director's job to actually bring the screenplay to life, but as a screenwriter your duty is to make the story playable on the page. You're a composer of story, character and theme. You're a visualiser of a narrative that's going to orchestrate a sense of emotion in the audience. And you can do that on the page. Don't just assume that the director will bring everything to life; that your job is to lay down only the basic foundations of the screenplay. Yes, you're writing the foundations of what will be made – a blueprint, to use another cliché –

but these foundations don't have to be basic. They should be anything other than basic! Compose the screen. Visualise your story, character and thematic intentions. Show us what you mean.

Charlie Moritz talks about scenes in a screenplay being like a dance, and that seeing the dance in your mind's eye can help to visualise the scene. This ties in neatly with the idea of structure and music, which has been articulated by various authors (including Zara and I). In essence, if you think about structure – of either the whole screenplay or individual scenes – as music, then you'll start to 'hear' the rhythm and tempo that the story needs, which will help you with plotting and writing action and dialogue. It'll also help you to find the emotional beats of your structure; where and when you want your audience to feel happy, sad, surprised, etc. The idea of a dance also works here to give you a visual sense of the rhythm and tempo of your story. Linked to the ideas presented below, if you can see your scenes playing out – the interactions of characters and their environments – then you're likely to focus-in on visual detail and paint a much stronger picture of what you're trying to say. Starting with dialogue and adding visuals later may work, but it's probably going to be harder. Start with the visual landscape of your screenplay and allow the images to move in your mind. Allow the story to dance.

VISUAL GRAMMAR

People often talk about visual grammar in screenwriting – even some script reports/coverage ask for assessors to talk about it – but what does it actually mean? Why do we put the word grammar – which belongs to language/linguistics – with the word visual? Well, it's all about the way a screenwriter composes the screen to elicit a specific meaning. Whether it's an action sequence, the use of an object in a scene, or even a character movement or gesture, it's a way of punctuating the screen (and, when writing, the page) so that it's understood in the way intended. Just like we use full stops, commas and paragraph breaks in writing – to give sense to the sentence or page – screenwriters employ visual techniques to do the same.

To help make sense of this, here's an example of how we might visually punctuate a scene – use the rules of visual grammar to give meaning:

```
EXT. HOUSE - DOORWAY - MORNING

Xavier strides up the path. He suddenly stops,
and takes a deep breath.

He raises his hand to press the bell, but hovers
his finger over it, unsure whether to press it.

A moment, then he lowers his finger and puts his
hand into his back pocket. He looks to the floor.

Another moment, then he looks up again. He stares
at the door before backtracking down the path.
```

As you can see from the underlining, there are a lot of specific actions here that help to give meaning to the scene. The scene could've been written in a line – but it would've been hollow and not really given a sense of Xavier's dilemma. Instead, by punctuating the scene with action and gesture – visual grammar – the scene comes to life and the reader (and actor) gets a much better understanding of what's happening in the scene.

Thinking like this is like thinking musically – to return to my earlier point. In other words, composing the screen through specific beats of action and gesture helps to give rhythm and tempo to the scene. This helps the reader to feel how the scene would play out, which also helps them to see the film in their mind – visuality from the page. If the example above had been written in a simpler way – like 'Xavier walks up to the door and hesitates, before turning back' – the scene would've had no rhythm, and therefore no proper understanding of character. Instead, because it's been composed almost musically – with specific 'notes' – it comes to life both on the page and in the mind.

Creative exercise

Play a piece of music and try to feel its emotions. If possible, block out the words and concentrate on the moods created by the music alone. Now visualise these moods and emotions and construct a visual scene or sequence to represent them. Think of the action as a dance. Allow yourself to see the characters and their actions, and how they interact with their environment (including what's in that environment). What does this dance look like? How might you write it as a screenplay? Is the meaning obvious enough without the need for dialogue?

SETTING

When you're writing a scene, you should always consider where it'd be best set. The location you choose – and what that location offers – can visually enhance the scene through context, conflict, tension and metaphor. Even in low-budget films, where there might not be the capacity to use extravagant locations, there's a lot to be said for thinking creatively about where you set your scene.

If you work out what the emotional beat or conflict of your scene is – what do the characters want and/or need – then you can brainstorm where to set it, thinking about how the location might help or hinder the characters – and, of course, add visual appeal to the screenplay. You should also consider how your characters feel in the location you've chosen, because that will affect how you actually write the scene. For example, are they comfortable or awkward? Do they want to be there, or get away? Are they trying to hide (physically or emotionally), or are they making the most of it? In a relationship, a particular location might be 'owned' by one of the characters – somewhere that makes them feel more at ease or in control than the other, giving us a nice power dynamic. Locations can also add spice to a scene or sequence, making it feel fresh and exciting. So, when deciding on the locations of your scenes, think about how one strong image can speak volumes about character, relationship, theme, pace and tone.

Creative exercise

For each of the following situations, think of a potential location that would bring out each of the following – **comedy**, **grief**, **romance** and **danger**:

- A family going on holiday
- A couple talking about their future
- A sports team in training mode

VALUED OBJECTS AND MOTIFS

A **valued object** is a physical item (object) that reappears several times (at least three) in the film's narrative to reflect theme, chart a character's physical and/or emotional growth, and sometimes provide humour (especially in the form of a twist). A **motif** is similar, but sometimes it's not really an object as such – it can be a recurring image, for example, perhaps more abstract in the sense that it's something we see but that's not necessarily part of the story (not referred to or used by the characters). Or, it can be something that a character does throughout the film – a repetitive action, movement or gesture. What both the valued object and motif do is offer visual symbolism and pleasure to the audience, who, recognising them, actively make meaning about their use. It's important to note that they offer visual pleasure as well as story symbolism because we must consider the audience and how they interact with a film – especially if we can conceive clever and credible ways of making them want to keep watching.

Here are some examples of the valued object in action:

- In *The Kids Are All Right*, the hat Paul gives Joni is important because it symbolises their bonding and her need for a father figure in her life. Later, when she's packing up to go to university, she leaves the hat behind, symbolising she no longer needs Paul, especially given all that's happened. Similarly, when Jules first goes to Paul's garden – the first time she sees him on her own – she's also wearing a hat. She uses it to cover herself up, symbolising her feelings of self-doubt. Later, when she starts to find herself and is more confident with who she is, the hat disappears and she shows her flowing red hair. Her hair is important here, too, because it's what reveals her secret affair when Nic finds it on Paul's pillow.

  The motorcycle is also a valued object. Paul, the 'interloper' of the story, has one and makes no bones about how good he thinks it is to ride. Contrary to this – which is narratively symbolic – Nic and Jules are very much 'anti-motorcycle'. As Paul's relationship with his kids develops, he gives Joni a ride home. This is important on various levels. Not only does it provide clear conflict – Nic isn't happy that Joni's been on the motorcycle – it symbolises a different world – Paul's world – that's beginning to encroach on the family, and that will lead to significant changes. For Joni as one of the film's protagonists, the motorcycle also allows her to try out something new, which symbolises her need to escape the control of Nic and become an adult in her own right.

- In *Leap Year*, Anna's much-loved Louis Vuitton case is symbolic of her character arc. It's characteristic of her organised, designer, capsule lifestyle, which we see her drop at the end of the film in favour of being less pretentious and with more freedom to explore herself. We see numerous scenes where, no matter what Anna's doing – from getting stranded on a beach to climbing a hill – she's pulling along her trusted LV case. She can't let go of it, like she can't let go of her structured life. The case, however, is stolen by a group of hoodlums, which metaphorically threatens her life – she can't live without it. But when Declan gets it back, putting his own life in danger by doing so, Anna's perceptions are suddenly altered and we sense that she and Declan will fall in love after all. This object is important, then, because, as well as revealing character, it provides a plot point that weaves itself into Anna's emotional arc.

Anna's apartment is also an important valued object because of its façade, which relates to her own life façade. We see it at the start of the film as the epitome of Boston living, and Anna's desperate to buy it with Jeremy. Her job as a lifestyle stager – making apartments look gorgeous so that they will sell – is also clearly important here. At the very end, though, Anna finally sees the façade of her life through the façade of the very same apartment – Jeremy's staged their engagement to get his hands on it – and she realises it's not what she wants anymore. Building up to this arc, we see a variety of very different places where Anna has to stay in Ireland. These include the small, cluttered and falling-to-pieces guest room at the pub-hotel in Dingle – which Anna manages to destroy – and the cramped room she has to share with Declan, where they pretend to be married. All of these work to provide a stark contrast with the apartment lifestyle she's used to, which, of course, she decides to drop at the end in order to move back to Dingle to be with Declan.

- In *Boy A* (scr. Mark O'Rowe, 2007), the trainers Terry gives to Jack in the first scene are important. Having just come out of prison, where inmates have to wear what they're given, Jack's now entered a world where he has choices. The trainers aren't therefore just functional – they're symbolic of his new life and freedom. They're also a nice metaphor for running – running away from the past and trying to start again. In a similar vein, shortly after this scene, Terry buys Jack food from a café, where Jack asks what a panini is. Again, this is only a small object – referred to, not actually seen – but it's important because, as well as inferring his backstory of being kept away from the developing world, it symbolises his new lease of life – a life of new experiences.

The recurring newspaper image of Jack as a child – as Eric – is used throughout the film to show us the torment that he's experiencing, unable to fully move on from what he did all those years ago. This is sometimes shown alongside a photo-fit of what the press thinks he'll look like now, complemented by the words 'Evil comes of age'. For the audience, this is quite ironic on various levels. Firstly, what we're seeing isn't what Jack looks like at all – to us, he's a vulnerable and gentle guy who's trying his best to start again. Secondly, the slogan 'Evil comes of age' means something different to us – we've seen him 'come of age', but not in an evil sense. We've seen him successfully reintegrate into society and develop a romantic and sexual relationship with Michelle – his first such relationship. This, therefore, goes against what's being suggested by the press, and in fact works really well to ask us hard questions about the situation – how do we feel, seeing Jack as we have as a character, not a media subject? Have we as the audience 'come of age' in our thinking?

And here are some examples of the motif in action:

• In *The Kids Are All Right*, Nic has a great love of wine. We see her drinking a lot, on numerous occasions, and sense that it's her outlet for the stress and worry that she seems to endure. She shares this love – and knowledge – of wine with Paul, though of course they're at odds for most of the film, so it never really connects them. When she eventually begins to warm to Paul, however, and undergoes the beginning of her emotional arc, she says no to wine and decides to stick with water – at which everyone is pleasantly surprised. Soon after, however, when she discovers Jules' hair in Paul's bedroom, Nic's world comes crashing down and she reverts to her love of wine – taking a big slug of it for all to see.

- In *Mysterious Skin*, we see the recurring image/action of Neil having fingers put in his mouth by men. This is set up early on in the story, during his first experience of being abused by the coach. The coach asks Neil to open his mouth, and, when he does, he puts a finger on the edge of Neil's mouth, making the whole thing appear very sexual. He takes a picture, which we see again later when Eric finds it in Neil's drawer. During Neil's first experience of prostitution, he grabs the man's hand and puts his fingers into his mouth. This clearly shows the effect his first experience with the coach had on him, and when we learn later that Neil feels emotionally scarred by the coach's disappearance – he thought he loved him – the fingers-in-mouth motif takes on a deeper meaning. As well as a sexual 'fetish', it appears to represent a feeling of belonging and possession for Neil – a sensation that he craves, in order to feel needed and loved.

- In *Boy A*, a running motif is that of Jack cowering in a corner, or at least moving himself away from people and objects. Whilst in prison, he would've invariably had very few possessions, and could've even been bullied by the other inmates. So, when we see him feeling sad and perhaps like he doesn't deserve to be in the outside world, he reverts to cowering away and finding his own space. As a motif, it reminds us of his painful emotional journey – his mixed feelings about whether or not he deserves a new life, given that he helped to take a life in the past. Furthermore, the motif is nicely juxtaposed whenever he's with girlfriend Michelle. He feels like he's finally reinventing himself when he's with her – like she gives meaning to his life – and so we see him always wanting to be close – cuddling, holding hands, visiting her at work, etc.

- In *Me and You and Everyone We Know*, Richard's hand bandage acts as a motif for his emotional arc. At the start of the film, he burns his hand – which he later tells us was an attempt to save his life – and, throughout, he wears the bandage. He later refers to it being covered up and not allowed to breathe – which reflects how he feels about his life. When he eventually takes the bandage off, there's a sense that his life's about to change. He even tells his sons that he needs to take his hand for a walk – it now needs to breathe. Relating this to the wider theme of the film, the bandage could be said to represent all of the characters who are suffocating in their lives, unable to be themselves.

  Digital objects and electricity also act as a strong motif throughout the film, reinforcing the idea of living in the digital age and being bound by technology. For example, Sylvie collects electrical kitchen equipment for her future life – she even questions the sales assistant about the future of electrical items. Peter and Robby are constantly on their computers, chatting to people they don't know and making pictures from typing out digital art patterns. Christine eventually has her work accepted for a digital art exhibition – it's a eulogy to her friend Ellen, replicating a foreign land with sound and image. And, at the very end of the film, Robby realises that the strange clicking noise he's been hearing throughout the film isn't anything to do with computers at all, like the adults have been telling him. The noise is in fact a human being – a man tapping his coin on the lamppost each morning as he waits for the bus. This is hugely symbolic of the idea of human interaction and touch – something lacking in a world of digital dominance.

Remember, then, that you're a screenwriter – someone who writes for the screen. Someone who tells stories through a visual medium. When you're developing your story's structure or writing one of your screenplay's scenes, try and see it first – try and visualise the character and the story, and then work out if, together, you can use them to visualise the emotion you're trying to convey. You might think about plot first, and how you can show your character trying to achieve something. You might then think about character traits, and how you can use action and gesture to represent their personality and drive. But then you should think about symbolism, and how valued objects and motifs can add visual and emotional texture to the story you're telling. Writing visually is about externalising and internalising – it's about showing us the surface, and also using the surface to show us what lies beneath, emotionally and thematically.

8. UNDERSTANDING GENRE

I want to start by saying that I hate genre. Or, I should say, I hate talking about and teaching genre. It's not because I don't think genre's important. And it's not because I don't like films that use genre. It's because it's such a big and difficult topic, and everyone who writes about it says something different, even contradictory. Apart from the often-used, and somewhat meaningless, statement, 'Genre is a French word meaning "type" or "form"...', writings on genre don't have that much in common. It means different things to different people, depending on their position in relation to film. Academics have certain views and delineations of genre. Financiers, marketers and distributors have different ones. Most writers have their own, devised to suit their practice. And some writers don't even think about genre at all. That's why I hate it.

But a screenwriting book that didn't talk about genre would be silly. Probably laughed at. So I need to say something. And I will! I could write a whole book about genre – well, actually, no, I couldn't, but someone else could – so to capture all that it is in one chapter is going to be hard. For that reason, I'll just say what I think needs to be said, and angle it as much as I can towards the writer. After all, you're reading this book because you want to write a screenplay. You want to sell it, too, of course, but first and foremost you need to write it.

WHO IS GENRE FOR?

Over the past few years, I've talked to many students about what they think genre is, and why it's important for their practice. They usually come in thinking that genre's really important – and that they know what it is. When they leave, they've usually decided that they don't really know what genre is (apart from a French word meaning 'type' or 'form'), and that they're no longer sure how important it is to their writing (at least early drafts). I find this really interesting. And let me say that I've not pushed them to think this at all – it's what's naturally comes out of lively discussions and creative exercises.

One thing I do is split the class into three and ask them to consider what genre means for the following groups: audience; marketing and distribution; screenwriter. I assign one group to each third of the class, and ask them to consider questions such as: 'What does genre mean to this person?'; 'How does genre feature in this person's daily practice?'; 'How important is genre to this person's connection to a film?'; 'What elements of genre is this person working with, attaching themself to, or expecting?'. Broadly speaking, these are the results that come out every time:

- **Audience** – expectation; appeal; taste; value for money; having a certain feeling; trailers; mood; visual understanding; decision to watch/spend money; segmentation; lifestyle; personality. Importance of genre = <u>8 out of 10</u>.

- **Marketing and distribution** – audience figures; money; tie-ins; music; talent; luring; persuading; trailers; rules; restrictions; visual tropes and clichés; profits; guaranteeing returns. Importance of genre = <u>10 out of 10</u>.

- **Screenwriter** – principles to understand; rules to follow; elements to try and change; story shapes; character types; twisting expectations; getting a commission; attracting an audience. Importance of genre = <u>6 out of 10</u>.

Although I'm sure many people would disagree with what I'm proposing, there's no denying that this is what came up. These are the results produced by screenwriters. And, if we look at the screenwriter list, we can see that much of it relates to the screenwriter's ambitions – and fears – of getting their work produced. In terms of their actual writing practice, it doesn't seem to feature so heavily. And this is where there's a really interesting tension – between art and commerce; between process and practicality. Screenwriters feel that they need to hit certain genres in order to get produced – but are their senses of genre the same as those who produce and market the work, or is there still a frisson between the known and the unknown?

GENRE – OR STYLE, OR FORM?

Another dimension – or problem – of genre is the interchangeable terms that often accompany it, namely style and form. For example, we could argue that comedy isn't a genre, but a form. It's something that you add into or onto a type of story, such as a romantic comedy, or a comedy drama. Comedy as a genre in its own right might be problematic because, apart from humour, there's nothing that binds all comedies together – there are no set character or story types. But this then assumes the definition of genre to be something that describes a type of story and a type of character used to tell that story. I actually think this is a useful definition (and more on this later), but not everyone will agree. This is especially the case for those marketing such a film, who might brand it as 'This year's best comedy'.

Listed below are some of the most common genres that we hear about, as categorised by screenwriting authors, screenwriting websites, film funding guidelines and screenplay competitions. Have a look at the list and see what you think – before I say something more on it.

- Love
- Horror
- Epic

- Western
- War
- Comedy
- Crime
- Sports
- Science Fiction
- Fantasy
- Adventure
- Road Movie
- Social Drama
- Historical Drama
- Documentary Drama
- Biopic
- Mockumentary
- Musical
- Animation
- Redemption Plot
- Rites of Passage
- Coming of Age
- Rags to Riches

What did you think? Are these genres? Or are they a mixture of genres and styles and forms? Would you put all of these into the same category – or should they be split into separate categories? Because genre has become a catchall expression, it's easy to say, yes, these are genres. But if we think about them carefully, we can see that they're very different entities. They're all referring to different things – whether that's theme, story shape, character types, visual tropes, artistic style or form. For me, the easiest way of breaking the list down, and any list like this, is into two parts: story types (genre) and execution (form). The story type includes the kind of story that's being told (theme), the shape of the story (arc) and the type of characters we'd expect (cast). The execution includes everything else that's specific to the film – including plot (specific structure), characterisation (execution, not archetype) and style (the way it's told – with humour, through song, as animation, etc). In summary then:

Genre = core story elements, including theme, story arc and archetypal cast design.
Form = execution of all of the above.

With this in mind, is it right to call the musical a genre? Do all musicals have the same core story elements? Think about *The Sound of Music* (scr. Ernest Lehman, 1965), *Chicago* (scr. Bill Condon, 2002) and *Nine* (scr. Michael Tolkin & Anthony Minghella, 2009) – are they all connected by similar themes, story arcs and character types? Or are they all just executed in the same way – through song and dance? Similarly, does the mockumentary sit well as a genre? What do *Drop Dead Gorgeous*, *Borat* (scr. Sacha Baron Cohen, Anthony Hines, Peter Baynham & Dan Mazer, 2006) and *Bruno* (scr. Sacha Baron Cohen, Anthony Hines, Dan Mazer & Jeff Schaffer, 2009) have in common apart from that they're a parody of a documentary? Do they, too, share themes, story arcs and character types? The answer, of course, is no. So I think we need to think about genre and form – about core story elements and execution – and how they work with and for each other, as opposed to merging them into one catchall phrase.

A good example of genre and form working together is the so-called road movie and rites-of-passage genres. To me, these are not two separate genres – they are a genre and an execution of a genre. Rites of passage is the genre, and road movie is the form. This is because rites of passage has clear genre elements in its fabric – the theme of transformation and being allowed to transform; a central character who needs to undergo a transformation in order to be cleansed or healed; and a central protagonist who usually has a mentor or series of mentors helping them. The road movie as a genre is difficult to grasp because, apart from the notion of someone travelling a road (or the land) to somewhere – execution – there's little else that binds all other road movies together. In this way, the road movie is an execution (form) of a story and character type (genre). Examples here include *Transamerica* (scr. Duncan Tucker, 2005) and *Due Date* (scr. Alan R Cohen, Alan Freedland, Adam Sztykiel & Todd Phillipps, 2010). Understanding the road movie as a form rather than a genre explains why it also works well for the coming-of-age genre. Because it's about execution and not core story elements, it's flexible enough to cater for different character types and different themes. As execution, it works well as a metaphor for the notion of travelling somewhere and arriving at a different place, regardless of the genre using it. Good examples here are *The Wizard of Oz* and *Stand By Me* (scr. Rob Reiner, 1986), both of which see young characters learning valuable lessons about life and about themselves before they're ready to go back home and face their families.

Creative exercise

Look at the list above and make your own connections between genre and form. Are there specific genres that suit particular forms well? If so, what's their relationship? Can you think of film examples of the two working together? Can you think of examples of forms that execute more than one genre well? If so, do you have any examples of these?

WRITING GENRE

Regardless of what you think genre is or isn't, there's one thing that remains constant – as a screenwriter, your job is to focus on the elements that you think make up your genre, and exploit them well. In doing so, you'll also be selectively keeping out elements that you think belong to another genre, and might dilute your story. For example, if you're writing a romance story, you probably won't want to write anything that alludes to the thriller – themes, character types, world, visual iconography, etc. You might like to combine the two – as with the film *Wicker Park* (scr. Brandon Boyce, 2004) – but, if you end up doing that, it should've been your intention from the start. Otherwise, you'll be taking all that you know about genre and applying it appropriately – bringing out the elements that will help your story, and taking away those that will make it lose focus and potential appeal to your target audience (if you have one).

That said, it's really quite rare these days to assign just one genre to a film. Not only are screenwriters mixing genres – which create hybrid- or sub-genres – it can also depend on what you see as important in a film, and what you think it's about. We all have different views and opinions, and this is no different when it comes to film. It's perhaps what makes some films more memorable than others – the mixing of genres to give new insights and surprises to an audience who probably have clear expectations of what the film is going to be from the way it's been marketed. Or is it the case that these films do still have one genre, and just different, innovative executions? Yes, that debate still goes on.

Let's look at two examples of films with hybrid genres (or forms).

• *Invictus* – on the face of it, this is a sports genre film. Why? Because the central story is about the attempts of a rugby team – and one player in particular – to win the 1995 Rugby World Cup. Like most sports films, the world that the team inhabits is symptomatic of the team's struggle, and provides hurdles that must be overcome in order to achieve success. In this case, it's the backdrop of a troubled South Africa. However, because the film focuses on Nelson Mandela's instrumental part in the team's success, does it make the film a biopic? In other words, a film that celebrates the life of an individual who goes out of his or her way to help others, and to initiate reform? Or, because Nelson Mandela is such an important figure in political history, is it a political drama, with rugby as the backdrop and metaphor? In this way, it becomes a film about the political struggle of an individual or a nation, seeking to instigate change and recognition of injustice. We could, perhaps, say that it's a political biopic executed through the world of sport. Or a sports film – Nelson Mandela assuming the archetypal role of the wise old man (coach) – set against a world of political change. In some ways it doesn't matter what we call it – it's a brilliant film that explores all these issues well. But if we're so adamant in the world of screenwriting to talk about genre, we might have a struggle on our hands. Which is why hybridity comes in handy.

- *Ratatouille* – according to most screenwriting literature, this would be classed as the animation genre. Why? Because it's animated, of course. That's true, but what does that actually tell us? Apart from the fact that what we see isn't real, but has been created by artists and technology, and that we might be presented with a world where anything can happen – including animals talking – it doesn't actually tell us anything. It doesn't tell us about the themes or the type of arc or even the kinds of characters we'll encounter. This is actually a rites-of-passage film. The story's about Remy, a young rat who ventures into a foreign place (the surface level of Paris) to follow his dreams of cooking great food, and who learns about himself and about friendship through his time with Linguini. Through this, he's also able to change people's perceptions about rats – not the stinking vermin that everyone thinks they are. In this way, then, the film is also (at least emotionally) a rags-to-riches story. The execution is animation – it couldn't be told any other way – but the core elements of genre certainly lie in the emotional arc of both Remy and humans. But from a marketing point of view, it's easy to see why it might be given the generic label of animation.

Hopefully, these examples give a clear sense of how and why genre is so difficult to grasp. And we must remember that genres change over time. Or at least their execution does. Some genres go out of fashion, and some genres come into fashion. Through hybridity, new genres or sub-genres emerge – depending on your definition of genre, of course. The way this comes about is through new things that occur in the world, which infuse the social and cultural consciousness. For example, would science fiction exist if it weren't for technological advances and people's experiences of them? Would we have biopics if the world of mass media and communication didn't exist, and nobody knew anyone outside their own town or city? Again, though, this is where the idea of form comes in. With new screenplays, are we really seeing genres being pushed, or are we in fact seeing the same genres but dressed up in different guises? Are the same core elements of a story – theme, character arc and cast design – being used again and again, but executed in fresh and surprising new ways?

Creative exercise
How might you use the topic of social media to tell a story in the following genres?

- Romance
- Thriller
- Crime
- Coming of age

Using the same genres, how might you use the topic of **global warming** to tell a story?

Using the same genres again, how might you use the topic of **financial recession** to tell a story?

There's no denying that, as a screenwriter, you're going to come into contact with the notion of genre at some point. Whether that's at the beginning or the end of the development process might depend on whether you're writing the screenplay on spec or on commission, and will almost certainly depend on you and your preferred ways of working. All I'll say here is that I think it's a really good idea to sit down and write a good, truthful screenplay in the first instance. Don't worry about genre – and maybe don't even think of it. Tell your story and then turn to genre later, when you're stuck or need someone or something to help you clarify exactly what it is you're trying to do. If you're lucky, you won't even have to think about genre. The producer, director, financier or distributor might do all that for you. Then you can just concentrate on telling a good story and making the screenplay true to your intentions. But then what do I know? I hate genre!

Finally, let me recommend some books that talk about genre in more depth that you might find useful. Stephen Duncan's *Genre Screenwriting: How to Write Popular Screenplays That Sell* (2008) is quite basic but useful nonetheless in identifying popular film genres and how to write them. Similarly, Ken Dancyger and Jeff Rush's *Alternative Scriptwriting: Successfully Breaking the Rules* (2006) takes an in-depth look at genre, exploring how to work with and against it. Also, from a structural point of view, Stuart Voytilla's book *Myth and the Movies: Discovering the Mythic Structure of 50 Unforgettable Films* (1999) examines how different film genres make different demands on narrative structure.

9. WORKING WITH THEME

As one of my students said recently in a presentation, theme is something that's painfully vague, yet we all know what it means. In other words, we know what it's getting at, and we know when we see, hear or feel it, but can we define it? What actually is it? It's a good question. The first thing to say, I think, is that theme is at the heart of all storytelling. It's what it's about. It's the core of the idea. It's the glue that holds everything together. It's what you remember. And it's what we're seeking when we engage in a story. But that's all very vague.

DEFINING THEME

The best way to define theme is to give examples. Examples of what it is, and what it isn't. This can be done in two ways, I think. Firstly, theme can be expressed by a word – or statement – that has imbued in it some kind of perspective, judgement or value. For example, someone might say that sex is a theme. But is it really? Sex might be a key part of a story – such as *Irreversible* (scr. Gaspar Noé, 2002), *Little Children* (scr. Todd Field & Tom Perrotta, 2006) and *London to Brighton* (scr. Paul Andrew Williams, 2006) – but what about it? How does sex here stack up as a theme? I'd argue that it's not sex per se that's the theme, but the kind of sex that we're seeing, or the view of sex that's being portrayed – sex as lust, sex as control, sex as loss of innocence, etc. In this way, sex becomes a motif for the theme

– a way of expressing it. What that expression of sex means – the perspective, judgement or value – is the theme. It's what it's about.

Here are some other examples of motifs and potential themes.

Motif	Themes
money	greed; corruption; desire; deceit; labour; ambition
gender	masculinity; femininity; gender politics; power; urge
religion	belief; power; morality; corruption
politics	power; corruption; justice; morality; governance
fashion	identity; perception; wealth; delusion; acceptance
food	greed; self-worth; body politics; inequality
technology	aspiration; ambition; power; control; fear

The motif, then, is central to expressing the theme, but it's not actually the theme. The motif closely relates to the world of the story, too, and possibly the genre. For example, money might be a motif that sits really well in a corporate world, or, depending on the story's need, in between the corporate world and the 'real' world. The film *Jerry Maguire* (scr. Cameron Crowe, 1996) is a good example. In this way, money-as-motif expresses the themes of greed, dishonesty and belief. Money itself isn't a theme.

Secondly, theme can be expressed as a question. Asking a question, which may indeed be provocative, can give a sense of the point of view that's going to be adopted in a screenplay, and therefore the theme or themes that it intends to explore. Such questions might be posed in a pitching document (for the reader), in the screenplay (spoken by a character), or in the marketing that surrounds the film's distribution (such as a strapline on a film poster). For example, the question 'Would you sell your soul?' – albeit metaphorical – conjures up possible themes of greed, dishonesty and given-up passions. Immediately, there's a bond between the idea and the audience because we get a sense of what it's going to be about. As another example, the question 'How do you know that your husband isn't a serial killer?' conjures up possible themes of identity, perception and betrayal. The question, therefore, can quickly and effectively target the heart of the piece you're writing, helping you and others to understand what it's really about.

Creative exercise

List the possible themes associated with these questions:

- When was the last time you helped an old lady cross the road?
- How far would you go to protect your child?
- Who do you know well enough to tell your darkest secret?

Now come up with a possible question for each of these themes:

- Misplaced lust
- Political corruption
- Social injustice

It's worth remembering here the distinction between the Central Dramatic Question (CDQ) and the Central Thematic Question (CTQ) of a screenplay. The CDQ is what drives the plot and the CTQ is what drives the emotion. Therefore, we might say that the motif you choose to express the CTQ can be woven into or pegged onto the CDQ. In other words, it's about finding where you can structurally place the motif to best bring out the CDQ. You don't want to overdo it, of course, but somewhere along the way you're going to need to remind the audience why they're watching this film. So weaving a single motif, or a set of them, into the narrative is bound to help reinforce the intention behind the film – what you're trying to say.

THEME IN ACTION

Because it's vague – at least until you know what it is – one of the best ways to understand theme is to watch films and read screenplays. You'll probably have to watch/read a couple of times before you truly understand the themes being explored and how they're being presented. And you'll probably have to watch/read a couple of times more to really understand how the screenwriter has crafted the screenplay to capture and express the themes – how they've designed the cast accordingly, or used motifs, or honed dialogue, etc. It might seem like an arduous task but you should try to enjoy it, learning something new each time. And the more you learn about theme, the easier it'll be to grasp – and, of course, to put into action with your own screenwriting.

Here, then, is a selection of films that explore poignant themes in interesting ways. I could've chosen any film to discuss how theme works, but I've tried to offer an appealing variety – a variety of themes, a variety of styles, etc – to demonstrate that, whatever screenwriting you're interested in, theme always sits at the heart of it and can always be expressed in interesting and insightful ways.

Me and You and Everyone We Know explores many themes, each relating to the idea of human connection – or the lack of it. Central themes include the loss of intimacy in contemporary society; the ruling power of technology, leading to the loss of intimacy; and the necessity of human touch. At its heart it's a film about what we've lost as human beings in today's world, and questions are asked about how we might recover this loss. The cast design helps to explore these themes. The characters we see include protagonist Christine, who, as well as wanting to find love, wants to find a physical outlet for her artwork; co-protagonist Richard, who's lost sight of what it means to be a father; and friends Heather and Rebecca, who desperately want to be adults and feel what it's like to be intimate with a man.

Other characters include Nancy, the art curator who's lost, lonely and spends her time chatting to people online; child Sylvie, who's planning ahead to when she has her own family; and Richard's son Robby, who finds himself immersed in online chat rooms. Together, the characters allow multiple stories to be told that express the same themes and concerns.

The actions and dialogue in scenes are also used to reinforce the film's central themes. For example, when Christine tries on shoes in the department store, Richard – the assistant – says that he's not allowed to touch her feet – he can only touch the shoes. This reminds us of the ludicrousness of contemporary law, and thematically reflects the impulse of the human to touch, to be intimate. This theme of touch and intimacy is also reflected when Robby strokes Nancy's hair; by Sylvie never being touched or held by mother; by Andrew writing notes to Heather and Rebecca because he's not allowed to go near or touch them; and the recurring problem of Richard not being able to touch anything properly because his hand's in a bandage. In the case of the latter, it's only when his bandage is taken off that Richard can truly experience intimacy with Christine, who wraps herself around him in the garden. Dialogue scattered throughout the film constantly refers to touch, holding, human connection and intimacy, perhaps epitomised by Nancy when proclaiming that e-mail wouldn't exist if it weren't for AIDS, and the fear of contamination and bodily fluids. This is ironic because, at the end of the film, the exhibition she curates is called *Warm: 3-D and Touch in the Digital Age*.

Grow Your Own (scr. Frank Cottrell Boyce & Carl Hunter, 2007) is a quirky British film that explores themes of racism and narrow-mindedness. The world has been chosen very carefully to explore these ideas – a traditional allotment in the North West of England – and the premise that the allotment is used to integrate and rehabilitate refugees couldn't be any more perfect. What this world and premise allows, therefore, is a cast of characters which provides conflict and tension for these themes to be realised – the old-fashioned and institutionalised British citizen, and the hopeful, wants-to-make-good foreign refugee. The film opens with a voiceover that describes the process of planting seeds in order for vegetation to grow, and the necessity of time and patience. As well as providing the backdrop for the film – the world of an allotment – this has clear thematic subtext about changing people's attitudes for the better. In an early scene, when one of the refugee's children asks if he can grow ochre in the allotment, the social worker replies, 'If you can make it grow, then yes.' Again, this line of dialogue works on a subtextual level – it's less about the ochre and more about opening up narrow-minded people's attitudes. Visually, the theme of racism and difference is epitomised by everyone agreeing to paint their sheds 'regulation red' – apart from Kenny, who's adamant that he's keeping his blue.

A strong theme explored in *Boy A* is forgiveness, and, relating to this, the idea of 'coming of age' – Jack coming of age in his new environment, where he's got the opportunity to be in control of his life and turn it around. These themes are reinforced throughout the film when Jack says, to himself and to others (Terry, Michelle, etc), that he's 'not that boy any more' – he's not a boy called Eric, but a man called Jack. His desire to bury the past and grasp the present – epitomised by the recurring words about him no longer being 'that boy' – provides a tangible plotline on which the themes of forgiveness and 'coming of age' can hang. What's interesting about this film is that, because of the controversial subject matter – a child killer being released under a new identity – its themes provoke a really strong moral question for the audience. The thing about theme is that it's something we can all understand and/or relate to, and feel – but, in the case of *Boy A*, it's something we all have to think very carefully about, and try to see from multiple perspectives. The central question that the theme elicits – should someone like Jack be able to bury his past and create a new life, without prejudice? – is very confrontational, especially when we think about it in the context of similar real-life cases. Thematically, then, it isn't an easy film at all, but it's what gives it a powerful social and political undertone.

Adaptation can be read as a story about disappointment. It's about the disappointment of life. This theme is depicted in various ways, through character, structure and dialogue. For example, Charlie is forever disappointed in himself, whether it's his inability to write the screenplay, his lack of guts to 'kiss the girl', or even his feelings towards twin brother Donald – disappointed that he's approaching screenwriting in a way he doesn't like (structure over meaning), and then disappointed that Donald's screenplay is going well and getting a great reception, unlike his own. In the story he's adapting, *The Orchid Thief*, Susan goes on the trail of the ghost orchid with John – which is set up as an important part of the narrative. When they finally see it, however – at the same time as being lost in the swamp – Susan says, 'It's just a flower.' Being disappointed with this – which juxtaposes with everything we've seen and heard about the flower before, through Susan's writing and John's descriptions – is reminiscent of Susan's feelings of self-disappointment, which we see early on in the screenplay (disappointed that she didn't defend John at the dinner party) and as she begins to arc (disappointed that she's allowed herself to follow a plain and simple life). Her words at the end of the film, 'I wanna be new... I wanna be new,' reinforce this theme – it's too late, and there's nothing anyone can do.

There's also another nod towards the theme of disappointment from Donald, who tells Charlie that he's not as happy as he might seem. He reveals to Charlie that he knew all along people at school laughed at him, and that in the end he simply learned to abide by a rule he set himself – 'You are what you love, not what loves you.' Juxtaposed with the apparently happy, frivolous lifestyle we've seen of Donald throughout the film, this brings to light a strong and surprising sense of disappointment in Donald's life – albeit with a strangely effective positive spin. And it's specific instances like this – brought out through character, structure and dialogue – that reaffirm the themes of a film and ask the audience to understand what the screenwriter's trying to tell them. To be touched in the way intended.

Creative exercise

Think about a screenplay you're working on and ask yourself what its themes are. What's it about? What are you trying to say? How are you trying to make an audience feel? Now go through the screenplay and consider how you're expressing the theme – what tangible elements of screenwriting craft are you using to bring out the meaning? You might want to use the list below to help you.

- **Character** – how does the cast represent the theme? What relationships existing between characters help to mirror the film's meaning?

- **Structure** – how does the physical journey bring out the emotional journey? Are there any specific plot points that you've used to nod towards the theme?

- **Visuality** – are there any valued objects or motifs that represent the theme? How does the landscape offer a visual backdrop that helps to amplify the film's meaning?

- **Dialogue** – do you use recurring lines or key phrases to reinforce the theme? Do characters speak about things in particular ways to help bring out thematic meaning?

10. CONSTRUCTING SCENES

A scene is a unit of action and emotion – of plot and character development – that's contained within one location and in one time frame. It's a space where characters act, react and make decisions, driving forward both plot and character arc, and, by association, theme. A scene is thus understood as a unit of **exchange** – a space where something happens, passes, moves on, etc. This is critical to consider because the fabric of a screenplay insists on progression – it's not about treading water and dwelling, but moving forward and developing. Even in scenes where characters reflect on what they've said or done, it's their character arc that's moving forward.

Scenes contain beats that move plot and character arc forward. These beats are micro elements of the story – a suggestion, a reaction, a movement, a decision, etc. Together, they build the scene into a unit of exchange – and that scene then connects with other scenes to make a sequence, a number of which culminate to make an act, which then bond to create the complete screenplay. So a scene is a crucial part of plotting the story you want to tell. When you break down your screenplay from the whole to the micro, you'll discover the scenes you need to make the story work. Remember, too, that a scene doesn't have to be complex or complicated – a scene can be four pages, but it can also be one line.

FINDING A SCENE'S PURPOSE

You might spend a lot of time plotting your script – index cards, step-outline, etc – so when it comes to writing a scene, you know exactly why it's there. Or you might enter scene writing with just a vague idea about what it's about, and why it needs to be in the screenplay. Either approach is valid, as it depends how you work. But what's necessary with both is that, at some point, you need to know exactly what the purpose is of the scene you're writing, so that you can understand it in the context of the whole.

Linked to what I say above about scene lengths, a scene might be very simple or very complex. It might, for example, simply give us information about what someone does next – an action, such as a telephone call, or a reaction, such as going home to cry. Or it might tell us a lot about the developing relationship between characters, which might shift and morph various times throughout a scene. For example, a scene might simply serve this function:

Karen tells Barry she's pregnant.

Or that might be the starting point of a scene, which then leads to more complex reactions, revelations and power shifts. For example, if we consider the 'baggage' that each character comes to the scene with – in other words, what's happened before and how they're feeling when they enter the scene – the scene might spark off multiple beats and numerous character arcs. If we keep with the example above, the scene might develop in the following complex ways:

Karen tells Barry she's pregnant… which jeopardises his plans to leave her – **because he's been having an affair, and was going to break up with Karen.**

This then makes Barry feel really uncomfortable – **because the reality of the situation has hit him and he can't think straight.**

Now there's an unborn child involved.

And so he decides to pretend he's happy, for now – **which as well as providing immediate conflict in that he's lying again, suggests further, darker conflict when, at some point in the future, he'll no longer be able to hide his true feelings.**

This makes Karen think her sister was wrong – **she thought he was having an affair and told Karen, which obviously distressed her a lot. And so now Karen's wondering why her sister said this – what was her motive?**

But it doesn't end there, because Karen actually isn't pregnant… she freaked out at her sister's news and thought this would be a good way of making Barry stay with her – **and so now both Karen and Barry are lying to themselves and to each other. The story's going to get very messy.**

In this example, then, both characters come into the scene with different agendas, are confronted with revelations and lies, and leave the scene with new agendas – and worries. They've both arced more than once in the scene – both have lied and then lied again, getting themselves into even deeper trouble, and both have developed different perspectives about the other characters in the story, the sister and the mistress. Although there's no conflict between them on the surface, there's deep conflict between them underneath – and with a clear indication that there will be even bigger conflict to come.

It's a good idea to think about the structure of a scene when you're writing and/or editing it. And when I say structure, I mean both its physical structure and its emotional structure. Like with the comparison to music I made in Chapter 6, the structure of a scene is also musical – it has inherent rhythm and tempo, carrying us along through its plot but also through its emotion. You might, then, ask yourself the following questions when structuring a scene, to help you find its purpose and the best way of getting that across:

- Where does the scene start emotionally?
- Where does it end emotionally?
- What's changed after the scene?
- What's the main conflict in the scene?
- What's the relationship dynamic / status / power in the scene?
- How does the relationship dynamic / status / power change as the scene progresses?

DRIVING A SCENE

It's really important, then, to know what's driving a scene. This is because it helps to sustain the flow of the overall narrative – when reading and when watching – and it can really keep the momentum going. Even if you don't know what your scene's about when you first write it, spend time considering it later so that you can get to the nub of it. Then, when you're re-writing and editing, you'll be able to strip it down, hone it and direct its focus towards what it's trying to do, which will stop it from feeling baggy, meandering and at odds with the story being told. Writing scenes is actually really hard, and one of the most common problems I've come across is that they're unsure of themselves – they're loose and unfocused. They often have a heart to them but it takes a while to get to it, and all that comes before and after the heart 'moment' feels like a generic set-up that could be in any screenplay, rather than a specific set-up that's relevant to that particular screenplay.

Creative exercise
Choose at least ten scenes from one of your screenplays and ask what's driving them. What are they about? What are they trying to achieve? Do you think they're achieving what you set out for them to do? If so, how? If not, how might you shape them so that they do?

Also look at the scenes that come before and after the scenes you've chosen. In the scenes you've picked, is there a sense that something's happened before? And is there a sense that something's going to happen afterwards? Is there evidence of the previous scene that's helping to drive the current one? And is there something in the current scene that's setting up the drive for the following scene?

Finally, ask yourself whether any of the scenes could be merged. Is there enough happening in each of the scenes, for example? Do any of them tread water – not moving forward but repeating the action and/or character development? What happens to the flow of your story if you merge some of the scenes?

INDUSTRY INSIGHT

Dr Marilyn Tofler, a Melbourne-based screenwriter, lecturer and script assessor – co-creator and co-writer of the television comedy *Whatever Happened to That Guy?* (2009) – has this to say:

Plot-driven comedy

One of the common problems that new writers face is not knowing what comes first – the scene or the plot. As writers, we shouldn't be thinking merely of scenes that are cool or funny, but how to write scenes that further our stories. I often find myself reading writers' scenes and thinking, 'Where are we going with this?' And then the end reveals the scene's purpose – a punchline that's possibly amusing, but doesn't have anything to do with the progression of the story.

Comedy needs to come out of the plot – not the other way around. A great screenplay is made up of more than just a load of interesting or funny ideas thrown together without purpose. There always needs to be an overarching idea or theme that governs every scene.

Rather than thinking 'Wouldn't it be funny if… ?', you should let the humour come naturally out of the story. Don't fall into the trap of using humour just because you think it'll get a laugh – instead, integrate it in a plausible and believable way. Remember the scene in *Bridesmaids* (scr. Kristen Wiig & Annie Mumolo, 2011) where Annie and Helen perform a toast-to-the-bride duel at Lillian's engagement? This scene was absolutely hilarious, as well as being totally plausible. It was obvious Annie and Helen were two girls battling it out in a public arena for 'best friend' status. This wasn't simply a way of getting a funny scene into the screenplay – it was a scene that was funny because it was a natural and truthful part of the story.

As an aside, don't be afraid to add humour to scenes with serious themes. You might even add humour to a dramatic or tragic screenplay to give the material an emotional lift. Always remember that comedy is truth – we use it in everyday life to survive the more unbearable aspects of living. Your screenplays can also become more bearable with the addition of comedic elements. In a more sombre or serious piece the humour will naturally resonate in a darker way, but will make your work more memorable. In *Thelma and Louise* (scr. Callie Khouri, 1991), for example, the screenwriter successfully weaves humour into a plot that revolves around rape, murder and thought-provoking challenges to gender stereotypes. In fact, when the film was released the screen previews barely touched on its more serious themes – the producers instead chose to show audiences clips of a fun and humorous female road movie. They were canny enough to know that humour sells – and feminism doesn't. The humour in the film ultimately made the serious issues more palatable.

In summary, then, don't be afraid to add a light or irreverent touch to your screenplays. But do ensure it comes from a position of truth within the story – be that truth of a character or truth of a situation.

© Marilyn Tofler, 2012

SCENES AND STORY TEXTURE

A film can really come alive with strong scene writing. The way a scene can move an audience – and a reader – shouldn't be underestimated. Obviously, what goes into a scene is really important – the characters, the action, the themes – but how those things are fused together in the scene is what can make a screenplay special. Scenes add to the overall audience experience of 'living' the story – they sculpt meaning into shape and allow it to be explored through action, dialogue and visual symbolism. When writing in a specific genre, it's how the scene plays out that really exudes the feel of the genre to the audience. It's the thrill of the thriller. The horror of the horror. The romance of the romance. By their nature and their texture, scenes pull audiences along with the story – up and down, in and out. They drip feed and they surprise. They shock and they scare. They reveal and they conceal. They shout and they whisper.

To give your scenes playable yet relevant texture, try to vary them in length. Don't, for example, give us three-minute scenes for the first half hour. Think big and think small – think complex and think simple. Carry us along by layering the pace through a combination of very short, short, medium and long scenes. Additionally, where you can, try to offer a mixture of interior and exterior scenes. Don't set things in specific places for the sake of it, of course, but on the big screen we like to see the epic and we like to see the intimate. Where appropriate, alternate the style and tone of scenes, combining them to give added dramatic texture – comedy followed by threat followed by flirtation, for example. And, as discussed in Chapter 7, think visually. Consider the potential for interesting, intriguing and meaningful visual texture that will bring the story to life on the page and on the screen. Whether it's location, action or some form of symbolism, deploy visual techniques to create a world and story that we believe through seeing.

The pace and feel of a scene also comes through careful crafting of its beginning and ending. The general rule is that scenes should start as late as they can, and end as early as they can. Rather than worry about formalities and setting a scene up, get straight in there – unless, of course, there's a specific reason why you need a slow build. And, when the scene's done what it's there to do, get out of it – don't hang around unnecessarily, feeling like you have to explain where the characters go next, how they leave the building, how they say their goodbyes, etc. As well as cutting down on screen time and production expense, this idea of 'topping and tailing' a scene also works to create pace and flow from one scene to the next. If you enter a scene late, such as where a conversation's already started, then it propels the audience to play catch-up and find out what's going on. Starting the scene at the very start of the conversation can feel slow and dry. Similarly, leaving a scene on a powerful action, emotion or line of dialogue not only propels the story forward, it punctuates for the audience how the scene's supposed to be read – how they're supposed to feel at the end of it. For example, ending a scene on the line 'He'd better watch his back' is far more threatening and meaningful than 'He'd better watch his back. Did you hear me? Right, let's go. Jason, will you drive? Cool.'

In later drafts of your screenplay, you might also want to think about the transitions between your scenes. This doesn't mean directorial transitions – wipe, fade, mix, etc – but story transitions, where how you end one scene and begin another – and even how you order scenes – creates a particular kind of feel or meaning. An example here would be one scene ending on a spoken question – 'Where's Kirsten?' – and the next scene beginning with a visual answer – 'Kirsten is swimming in the sea, naked except for a pair of goggles.' Another example – though be careful of being naff here! – would be one scene ending on someone picking up a bunch of keys, and the next scene beginning with someone throwing down a bunch of keys. If you're writing comedy then you should really think about scene transitions because, through them, you can create a lot of visual and verbal humour – using irony, repetition, exaggeration, surprise, etc.

WRITING SCREEN DIRECTIONS

As already discussed, some people think that a screenplay doesn't – or shouldn't – have any written style to it. It should read simply as an outline. On the contrary, a screenplay has as much work to do on the page as it does on the screen. A script has to be read as a story – as a text in itself – before it can be commissioned, and so it's important to write in an appealing and stylistic way to convey the feeling of the story. How a reader feels about the story will directly affect their decision to commission or recommend it.

When writing screen directions, thinking about the minutiae of a scene in four simple yet effective ways can help you to enhance the feel of a scene enormously. These elements are pace, action, visual landscape and layout.

We talk a lot about **pace** when writing screenplays, but this is usually in reference to the whole drama as opposed to specific scenes. For example, we talk about using visual sequences and juxtaposing story threads to create a kinetic flow. But writing scenes is also about pace. It's about structuring and writing the movement and flow of a scene to mirror the feelings we anticipate of our reader.

For example, consider the difference between this:

```
Mary is sitting in her living room, looking at the
clock intermittently, waiting for Simon to return home.
```

And this:

```
Mary sits.

And sits.

The clock ticks.

She looks up, intermittently, waiting.
```

Although both screen directions give exactly the same information, the first is arguably quite bland and detached from the character of Mary. The second is more evocative of the pain Mary's enduring as she waits for Simon. Writing the screen direction in beats that mirror the character's inner turmoil gives a stronger sense of the how the scene is supposed to feel, and the pace of how it'd be played out if produced.

When thinking about the action of a scene, a simple exercise in evaluating how verbs are used can really enhance the power of a scene. Here, the intention is to create a more accurate sense of how a character does something – and, by association, also create a stronger sense of the visual composition of a scene.

You should highlight all the verbs used in your screen directions and, thinking about the context of the scene and the characters in it, ask yourself whether more suitable verbs will create a better understanding of the scene. For example, the difference between `Marco walks`, `Marco strides`, `Marco saunters` and `Marco minces` is more than pure linguistics. The verbs here all tell the same basic action, but each one very specifically defines his character. Similarly, `Emma laughs` doesn't really tell us anything when we compare it to `Emma cackles`, `Emma giggles` or `Emma sneers`.

Although specific directorial shots are best avoided in a screenplay (close-ups, pans, etc), screenwriters can allude to them by carefully describing scenes to evoke a sense of the **visual landscape**. It's like you're composing the screen – as a director would – through subtle written detail rather than literally calling the shots. So, if you're envisaging specific camera angles as you write, try and evoke them through description that will direct the reader's mind to the intended visual landscape.

For example, if a horror requires a close-up of a knife blade very close to the victim's face, then an expression like `The blade reflects in the pupils of her eyes` clearly suggests this. Similarly, `The horses gallop across the plain, the sun` `sinking behind them` suggests a long, wide shot that uses the whole frame. Not all screen directions need this amount of detail, of course, but consciously thinking in directorial ways will help you to enhance the visuality of your scenes.

As has already been alluded to above, the **layout** of screen directions can affect how they're read and therefore experienced. The general rule-of-thumb in screenwriting is that a direction shouldn't run for more than four lines before a paragraph break's inserted. But, in many cases, it can be a lot less than this. It can be useful to look at the layout of a poem and ask why the text's broken up in such ways, to elicit emotion and meaning. This can then be fed back into writing screen directions.

You might want to play around with the layout of your screen directions by first of all making each one as short as possible, and then each one as long as possible. Looking back at the two versions, with their different levels of pause (the white space between paragraphs), consider how the feel and tone changes in each. Linking this back to the context of the scene – where does it fit in the grand scheme of things, and what's its purpose? – you should ask yourself what's been gained and what's been lost by changing the layout. This will then help you to decide which would work best for your scene.

Creative exercise

Using one of your own screenplays, deconstruct some of your screen directions by following the advice given above. You might want to look at sections of direction through the four different lenses – pace, action, visual landscape and layout – before bringing them together to understand how they're working as a whole. Try to be as brutal as you can when making changes, if not to create something new then just to let you see how differently things can work. When you've done this, compare the old and new versions and evaluate how much more – or less – effective your screen directions have become.

INDUSTRY INSIGHT

Screenwriter, script consultant and coordinator of screenwriting at San Francisco State University, Julian Hoxter, author of *Write What You Don't Know: An Accessible Manual For Screenwriters* (2011), has this to say:

Writing the action sequence

Writing action sequences is a tricky thing to do. Every writer has their own approach and style, and also different kinds of movies require different levels of detail. Famously, Shane Black – *Lethal Weapon* (1987), *The Last Boy Scout* (1991), *The Long Kiss Goodnight* (1996), *Kiss Kiss Bang Bang* (2005) – used to add in ironic or factual asides about the type of gun his hero was using, or the way he expected industry readers to respond to his scenes. But don't copy Shane Black – invent your own style. Though you might follow his advice in this at least: 'The worst of the action films are the ones where everything is one shout from beginning to finish. And there's no differentiation between beats, like small or big, or quiet or expansive. It's all just one loud shout.'

Remember that **narrative economy** should always be in the back of your mind as you're writing any sequence. Say as much as you can in as few words as possible. Here are a few thoughts to get you started:

- **Clarity** – whatever your genre and level of technical complexity, you have to find a way of hitting a balance between blandly over-simplifying and When Details Attack. That is a nice judgement, of course. One can't really generalise other than to say: you're writing a story, so, if in doubt, make sure story trumps detail.

- **Flow** – that means you have to keep the narrative flowing throughout. Don't let the pace of the read drop away through over-writing or you'll lose the very excitement an action sequence should be all about. We need to be focused on why we're watching action at least as much, if not more than, what we're watching. I'm all for cool explosions, but they don't fill my heart with movie love on their own.

- **Character** – the way to make sure narrative flows through action is to play that action to character. Action happens because our characters initiate it, or are the victims or objects of it. That means we should care about what happens to them. Don't hide them behind props and special effects. Every action scene should be led by character and should speak directly to their arcs and relationships. The characters involved will use, perhaps even discover, skills and take decisions in ways that tell us something about who they are, where their thinking is, what their strengths and weaknesses are, and what they're trying to do in the larger story.

  This applies both in modest and multi-million dollar sequences. If you compare the set piece action sequences from *The Avengers* (scr. Joss Whedon, 2012) to the *Transformers* movies (2007, 2009, 2011), for example, you'll see a far greater emphasis on character and story development through action in the former than in the latter.

- **Justification** – the way to make sure you're being honest with your audience and focusing your action through character is by making sure your action sequences have weight. In other words, you need to justify them through story, not just have them ambush the plot. This helps to create a deeper resonance with the plot.

Of course there's a great deal more to say about how to structure action sequences as spectacle. All I'm trying to do here is to give you a framework for your thinking to keep you honest to your overall story goals while you write. Always try to avoid writing action for action's sake, but revel in the kinetic, dramatic fun you offer us when you write action well.

One final note – when writing action sequences in a spec script, **white space is your friend**. Don't write in big, dense paragraphs, crammed with detail. Encapsulate a moment of kinetic drama in a sentence or two, leave a blank line, then give us the next. It makes for a faster, more exciting read – and you want industry readers to be your friends!

© Julian Hoxter, 2012

There's a lot to be said about writing scenes, then. Far from being functional entities that hold everything together – character, action, dialogue, visual metaphor, theme, etc – they're special spaces where careful thought, crafting and honing can build something special that serves the screenplay in many ways. As well as allowing action and character development to take place, scenes can – and should – provide dramatic texture that works with the rest of the story. They can, for example, build pace and allude to emotion. They can serve genre and style. They can also, through their structural composition, create a sense of meaning that's more than the sum of their parts. Scenes, then, aren't merely functional – they're visceral. They draw you into the page or into the screen and make you think, feel and believe.

11. WRITING DIALOGUE

Many people think that writing dialogue for screenplays is easy. It's just writing how people talk, right? Well, like most perceptions about screenwriting, this isn't really the case. It's a lot more complex than that. As screenwriters, the challenge is to make what characters say sound realistic, whilst carefully plotting and crafting dialogue so that it fulfils a number of functions – advancing plot, defining character, revealing relationships, hinting at themes, referring to the story world, etc. It's about being naturalistic, not realistic – an illusion of reality, brought about by dialogue that's naturalistic yet highly polished. Realistic would be something like this:

> SIAN
> Hey babe. How are you? Did you
> have a good night?

> GRACE
> Yes, thanks. You? I missed
> you… where did you get to?

> SIAN
> Oh, I was knackered. Sorry.
> Those night shifts have taken
> it out of me.

> GRACE
> That's ok. As long as *he*
> didn't call you again!

> SIAN
> Don't worry, I'm not falling for
> that again. He's such a creep!

> GRACE
> Not to mention a total loser.

Naturalistic, on the other hand, is something like this:

> SIAN
> Hey babe. Good night?

> GRACE
> Yeah… but where were you?

> SIAN
> Knackered, sorry. It's those
> night shifts.

> GRACE
> As long as *he* didn't call again!

> SIAN
> Not falling for that again.
> What a creep!

> GRACE
> Not to mention total loser.

The difference, as you can see, isn't so much about voice as it is about tight, focused, meaningful conversation. The realistic version is flat, functional and very baggy – in the sense that everything's given a proper lead in ('Oh', 'That's ok', 'Don't worry', etc), as if we need the full conversation to make sense of everything. The naturalistic version sounds the same, but it's been polished – sentences are not full and proper ('Knackered, sorry', 'Not falling for that again', 'Not to mention total loser', etc), all the baggy lead-in expressions have been taken away, and there's a greater sense of character dynamics, rather than them appearing to be on a level playing field. It also has pace and texture, rather than being dry and 'nice'.

It's useful to think of dialogue as an exchange, not merely words on a page that a character will speak. What I mean by this is:

- **Who's the character really talking to?** Is he talking to his father or, by doing so, is he really talking to his mother, who's hovering in the background? What's he saying to his father, and how is it really aimed at his mother?

- **What does a character really want – or need – to say?** When she arrives at his office, what's on her mind? Why has she gone there today, for the first time since they got married? How does he feel having her there?

- **What does a character feel they can't say, and why?** Why can't she tell her how she feels? What's stopping her? What's she talking about instead, to cover up the fact that she can't say what she feels?

- **Who's present in the scene, affecting what can or can't be said?** Why does the conversation change when he enters the room? How does the subject continue to be discussed, but in a roundabout way? How do the others feel about things being spoken about like this?

- **What's repressed (unsaid) rather than expressed?** Why aren't they talking? Why are they just eating, and not chatting like everyone else around them? Do they both know there's tension lurking beneath their situation?

By thinking of dialogue as an exchange, and not just spoken words that are functional for the scene (what's often called 'on the nose'), you'll start to inject life into your scenes. For one thing, you'll start to think about silences – what's not said – and how they might say more than actual words. Not only that, but by thinking about what underscores a scene – tension, conflict, humour, etc – your dialogue will be anchored to the key intention of the scene, rather than just free-flowing talk that goes nowhere. Also, you'll think more about character dynamics, and how dialogue – or silence – can reflect the relationships between characters. All of this will give your dialogue texture and pace – which is very appealing to read and hear.

> **Creative exercise**
> Take one of the key points above, and the example situation, and write a scene that explores the key point being made. Don't worry too much about the characters you choose, or the specific context the scene's surrounded by – just write a scene that explores through words (or silence) how dialogue's much more than just words on a page.

STRIPPING DOWN

As I've already mentioned, writing good dialogue is about constantly honing and trimming and stripping lines down to their minimum. There are exceptions, of course, where you want a character to be verbose and flowery in what they say – but, even then, it's about embellishing in specific ways and choosing the exact vocabulary that reflects the character and situation. But, generally speaking, writing dialogue is about writing as little as possible yet still giving the meaning. There are some simple tools to consider when writing and editing dialogue.

Firstly, here's a list of very common **redundant words** found in early draft screenplays. By redundant, I mean words that don't really add anything to what's being said, apart from the time needed to speak them and the paper needed to host them. Also, they're common expressions we use in our daily lives – realistic – but, as we're aiming to be naturalistic, they can actually be a nuisance. They clog the page up and slow down the reading experience.

- Oh
- Well
- So
- Ok
- Umm
- But
- Yes
- No

This isn't to say that screenwriters can't use these words in their screenplays – of course not – but rather that it's usual to cut them out and speed up the pace of the dialogue. This is important not just for how it will translate to the screen, but for the reading experience, too. As I've already mentioned, reading a screenplay should be an experience in itself, and sharp, economical, textured writing is one way to help achieve that. Also, it's common that if an actor can't express these words visually (a facial expression, a gesture, etc), they will ad lib anyway.

Secondly, here's a list of very common **expressive words** found in early draft screenplays. By expressive, I mean words or phrases that directly mimic someone's internal reaction to a situation, which can – often – sound wooden and clunky. We have to remember, too, that we're writing for a medium where we see the action take place, and actors can pretty easily visualise expressive words and phrases.

- Really?
- No way!

- It can't be...
- Oh my God!
- Yes please.
- She said what... ?
- He did what... ?
- This can't be happening!

Again, it might be entirely appropriate for a character to speak such lines – but more often than not they're either superfluous or clunky. Think how actions might be better at expressing these internal reactions – give a character something to do instead of something to say. You might find that, as you get to know your characters better, their internal logic, and the way they physically react to situations, becomes clearer and more interesting.

Creative exercise
Choose three of the expressions from the list above and think of ten ways that each could be expressed visually. If you're already working on a screenplay, and have draft scenes available, go through the dialogue and see if there are places where you can replace expressive words with character actions. Ask yourself this – what do the replacements add to the feel of the screenplay?

Thirdly, another common problem in early draft screenplays is that characters seem to repeat themselves, even within the same exchange. It's as if screenwriters feel they need to make it really clear what's happening, and worry that a character saying it just the once might not work. Here's an example:

                    TONY
        I don't like it there. It's not
        my scene. I'll give it a miss.

Essentially, these three short lines are all saying the same thing – that Tony doesn't like the place someone's talking about, and therefore won't go. If he said just one of these lines, the meaning would still be clear. Each line has a different flavour, of course, but they're not adding anything to the conversation when repeated like this. So, if Tony's friend is asking him if he wants to go to a bar that's recently opened, saying 'I don't like it there' means that he's unlikely to go. 'It's not my scene' also tells us this – the implication is that he doesn't want to go. What this exchange is really about is a rejection of an offer – 'I'll give it a miss' – and so, in this example, it's as if the decision needs to be repeated three times before it's understood. Or as if the first two lines are lead-in lines for the actual answer – 'I'll give it a miss.'

Here's another example, this time from a character expressing her excitement about a potential new partner:

JODI
I'm so excited about him. He makes me feel really good. He gives me the tingles.

Again, all these lines are essentially saying the same thing – that she's excited, and feels really happy with her new partner. When you read them all out, as part of the same exchange, they sound wooden, on the nose and, quite frankly, cheesy. And that isn't good. Choosing just one – maybe two – lines, and carefully honing them to pack in as much information as possible, makes the dialogue richer and more powerful.

CHARACTER VOICE

Another problem – and this is a big problem! – with early drafts is that characters lack a strong sense of voice. Many screenwriters think that they've given their characters a voice, but when you read the dialogue it's actually pretty voiceless. Some people talk about covering up the character's name on the page, and being able to tell who speaks a line from the line itself. I don't think this actually works all the time, I have to say, but, nevertheless, it gives you a good idea about the purpose behind making characters distinguishable from one another. One of the main reasons characters lack a sense of voice is because the screenwriter isn't listening to the world. You really do have to listen to people – different people – and understand how they verbalise themselves.

When considering character voice, and what drives it, it's useful to think about the following points:

- **Personality** – how is dialogue driven by your character's personality? What makes someone tick, and what makes them speak the way they do? Can we tell who your character is just from what they say?

- **Attitude** – what's your character's attitude towards the world and other people? How would they vocalise this? Even when they don't think they're being particularly vocal, how do their beliefs and points of view creep through?

- **Preoccupations** – what does your character like to talk about? What don't they like to talk about? What's their world and how does it influence what they talk about? What bugs them, or intrigues them, or excites them?

- **Intelligence** – how intelligent is your character, and how does that influence their dialogue? Do they feel comfortable talking about certain things? How do they talk about things – confidently, naively, unfairly, etc?

- **Profession** – is there a particular language associated with your character's job? How do people in that workplace talk, and how does this affect your character when he or she isn't in the workplace?

- **Lifestyle** – where does your character live? Where were they brought up? Is there something about the life they lead – through choice or force – that affects the way they talk? How is the world reflected through dialogue?

From this list, you can see how closely dialogue and world are related – the world that your character's living in, and the world that they've created for themselves, which may be internal.

Notes on a Scandal offers a great case study of character voice with respect to the brilliantly crafted dialogue of its embittered protagonist, Barbara. I've already discussed how the world of the film is depicted, and voice is another key element of this. The world is voiced through Barbara. Her character voice not only defines her personality, it defines her world – or at least the world that we see through her eyes. Her dialogue is far from incidental. It stretches way beyond functionality to give us a vivid sense of her personality, attitude and worldview. We hear her talk horribly about her colleagues – 'limp little Brian' and 'fatty Hodge, the pig in knickers' – and pessimistically about her students – amongst them 'doubtless the odd terrorist', trading 'wank mags' and academically performing 'above the level of catastrophe'. Throughout the film, her dialogue becomes more acerbic and dark. Examples of her polluted words and phrases include – 'minefield', 'toxic waste', 'dead', 'knives', 'Judas had the dignity to hang himself', 'furtive', 'solitude', 'chronically untouched', 'crack cocaine' and, as Sheba calls her, 'waste and disappointment'. To reiterate the point, this isn't incidental. The dialogue has been crafted and honed to a point where everything Barbara says reveals something about her life and her world.

I've already given a sense of how important dialogue is to *Juno* in the discussion of worlds – how the topic of conversation and vocabulary characterises the world, or gives a voice to the world. It's definitely a film worth watching to get a lesson in writing dialogue – not just for world but also for character, each one having their own clearly defined voice. Some people find the voices irritating and surreal, but, taste aside, there's no doubt that they draw attention to the need for distinctive character voice in a screenplay. Here are some examples:

- The shopkeeper, watching Juno shaking the pregnancy testing kit to try and make it change its result: *That ain't no Etch a Sketch. This is one doodle that can't be undid.*

- Juno's friend Leah, answering the telephone: *Yo, yo, yiggity yo.*

- Stepmother Bren, who, after waiting in suspense, is told that Juno's pregnant: *I was hoping she was expelled, or into hard drugs.*

- Juno herself, realising that her waters have broken: *ThunderCats are go!*

Creative exercise

Write a scene where two people discuss euthanasia. The two characters you should use are Brenda, a 50-year-old counsellor who's got a PhD in psychology, and Sean, a 20-year-old shop assistant who only watches reality TV. This isn't an exercise in stereotyping – it's intended to get you thinking about character voice, and how someone's background and worldview directly influences what they say and how they say it.

SUBTEXT

Screenplays with lots of on-the-nose, expositional dialogue are boring and hard to engage with. They don't encourage any sense of participation, and make it really hard to gauge character dynamics and relationships. That's because people say exactly what they mean and feel, leaving no room to read between the lines or try and work out the subtext. In essence, then, subtext is about the 'unsaid' – or the 'what else is said'. In other words, it's about people not answering a question, or changing the subject, or misunderstanding what's being asked. Subtext encourages an audience to play a game, trying to work out what's really going on. And what's going on usually relates to control, power, tension, relationship or comedy.

Take the following situation as an example:

- Lucinda and Jeremy have been on a date. Jeremy really likes Lucinda, but isn't sure if she feels the same. When they get to where his car's parked, he uses the car as a way of testing her feelings for him. He gloats about the colour, and asks Lucinda what colour cars she likes. He tells her that it's really economical – diesel – and tries to get her views about the kind of engine she prefers. He tells her that he wishes he'd bought a three-door, not a five-door, and that he's considering buying a roof rack. Finally, he asks her whether she prefers to drive or be driven.

Although this situation might seem silly, it's perfectly normal to see this kind of thing in a film – either as a comedy (which this situation might well be), or as a more serious, measured attempt to get to the truth of a situation. What's important is that there's something going on beneath the words – something that someone's trying to imply, or discover, or that someone else is trying to avoid or run away from.

Here are some examples of scenes that might be driven by subtext:

- Someone talks about their love of classical music to make someone feel inferior.

- Someone discusses politics to hide the fact that they're unemployed.

- Someone speaks highly of their neighbour to gauge whether or not their partner's been having an affair with them.

- Someone purposely misunderstands a question in order to divert from the truth.

Characters talking about one thing and meaning another – whether it's for comedic effect or to reveal something about character relationships – also works really well when it's used in relation to something visual going on in a scene, such as the use of an object or the way characters move around each other (the 'dance' of a scene). For example, in the situation above, the car works as a really nice symbol of everything Jeremy's talking about. He might even interact with it, as a way of testing whether Lucinda will as well – which might then tell him more about her feelings for him. In this way, both dialogue and visual landscape help to build the tension of the situation, enticing the audience to play along. Think how these other examples might work:

- Two characters are flirting at the same time as painting a shed.

- Two characters are trying to threaten each other at the same time as wrapping Christmas presents.

- Three people are trying to work out who killed their friend at the same time as cooking a meal.

- Three characters are hiding their feelings of grief at the same time as trying on clothes.

Sometimes subtext comes naturally when you write a scene – you know what you want to get out of it, and have ideas about how you can be playful with the language. But sometimes you have to really work at subtext, and see when a scene has the potential to be richer, subtler and more complex. In this case, you might have to stand back and ask what the scene's about, as well as working out where the characters have come from and where they're going. On occasions, it takes someone else – such as a script editor or director – to point out the potential for subtext in a scene. It might be that you've spent so long working on a scene that you've lost sight of what it's trying to do. And, of course, subtext shouldn't be forced. It's no good giving a scene subtext if it doesn't need it, or if it feels too staged. Good subtext feels natural and true to where the characters are in the story. It should add dynamism to the characters, the scene and the pace of the story, and tell us something interesting – or funny – that we didn't already know.

Linda Seger's book, *Writing Subtext: What Lies Beneath* (2011), is the first book of its kind, dedicated purely to writing subtext for the screen. It's certainly worth checking out to see what's said about writing subtext into dialogue.

Creative exercise
Choose one of the situations listed above, and write a scene based on it that uses subtext. Re-draft it a few times until you think it's doing what it needs to. Then show it to another screenwriter or friend, and ask if they can work out what the subtext is.

THE KEY PHRASE

Many films make use of the key phrase – a sentence, or sometimes just a word, that's repeated throughout the story (usually at least three times) to do one of the following:

- Clarify a theme (the controlling idea)
- Reflect a character's physical journey (what they're doing)
- Reflect a character's emotional journey (why they're doing it)
- Provide humour (something we expect from a character)
- Provide a twist (if the sentence or word changes, usually at the end)

Like the visual motif, the key phrase is a clever reminder from the screenwriter to the audience about what they should be thinking, feeling and understanding. As we can see from the list above, it clearly relates to the character's voice (what do they say and how do they say it?), and also branches out to do more: clarify theme, reflect their journey, etc. Used wisely, this small 'trick' can give the audience a lot of pleasure.

Here are some examples of the key phrase in action:

- In *Boy A*, Jack (new identity) repeats the phrase 'I'm not that boy' (Eric, his former identity). This clarifies the protagonist's desire to re-create his identity, and convince himself that he does deserve another chance now that he's served his time. It also works as a juxtaposition with everything that Jack sees in the press about himself – 'Evil Comes of Age'.

- In *Strictly Ballroom* (scr. Baz Luhrmann & Craig Pearce, 1992), Scott, Fran and Doug all use the phrase 'Live your life in fear'. This has clear thematic resonance, especially considering the revelation that Doug never danced with Shirley in the finals – Barry convinced her to dance with Les (so that they'd lose). With Barry as the oppressive antagonist to many of the film's characters, this key phrase also reflects the world that they're living in.

- In *Juno*, Bleeker shows his naivety about the world when, after Juno says she's going to have a baby – the actual physical thing, after nine months of pregnancy – he says, 'That's what happens when our mums and teachers get pregnant.' This line is later repeated to him by a friend, also referring to Juno's baby. As well as providing great humour, this line reinforces the naivety of the characters who've found themselves in a situation that's beyond their years – getting pregnant.

- In *Ratatouille*, the phrase 'Anyone can cook' is repeated several times by several characters. The phrase belongs to famous now-dead chef Gusteau, coined by him in one of his books, but is now repeated by Remy, Linguini, Skinner and Colette – as well as other secondary characters. The phrase works on a micro level (nobody thinks Linguini can cook, for example) but it's more powerful on a macro level as it reinforces Remy's struggle to gain recognition for the rat community. The odds are against him – how can a rat cook? – but inspired by Gusteau's mantra, he proves himself and his fellow rats by making a success of the ailing restaurant.

KEY LINES

As well as key phrases, most films have a few key lines of dialogue. This is pretty subjective, actually – different people pick up on different lines – but often they stand out as being important, at least on a subsequent viewing. You could say that films have many key lines, in the sense that all the dialogue's been crafted and polished to fulfil various functions, but true key lines are the ones that tell us something much more than the context they're spoken in. They're sometimes repeated, too, though in a different way from the key phrase – they might be alluded to, for example, rather than being repeated in an overt way. The best way to understand key lines is to give a raft of examples.

When Paul arrives at Nic and Jules' house in *The Kids Are All Right*, he asks how long they've lived there. Jules says that it's been ten years, then realising this, says to herself, 'God, has it been that long?' This is an important thematic line as it relates to the problems Nic and Jules are having – their relationship's turned stale, and Jules has lost her vocation in life, not knowing who she is any more. This line then relates closely with Jules' speech to Nic, Joni and Laser towards the end of the film – after the revelation of the affair – where she says that marriage is a hard slog, and that, after a while, you stop seeing the other person. Just like you stop remembering how long you've been in a place.

In another scene, Paul and Laser are playing basketball. They discuss what they'd prefer – to be buried or cremated. Paul says he wants to be buried – to be remembered – whereas Laser thinks it's better to be cremated. As well as highlighting the fractures in their relationship that will become even clearer later, the topic of conversation is rich in metaphor and meaning. For example, Paul's desire to be buried matches his love of organic food, growth and the natural world. This, in turn, draws further parallels with Jules – who he's now sleeping with – who's in fact made the family start composting (which Nic criticises to their friends). Furthermore, the fact that Laser's more like his mother, Jules, than he is Nic – but here shows a preference that's much more 'Nic-like' – suggests that he's also undergoing a character arc, and is in fact trying, albeit subconsciously, to reconnect with his true family, not 'interloper' Paul.

At the very start of *Leap Year*, Anna describes her job at the Davenport Cooperation as that of a lifestyle 'stager' – 'Nobody knows what they want until I lay it out before them.' As well as telling us what her job is, which ultimately reflects her false, shallow personality, this line is also an important foreshadowing of the emotional journey that she'll undergo throughout the film – learning to see beyond the surface and understand what people really need, not merely want. She even says this about herself later in the film, when she returns to Dingle to announce her love for Declan – 'She had everything she wanted, but nothing she needed.' This is a clear emotional punctuation mark to the end of the story, reminding the audience what the film – and her journey – has been about.

Notes on a Scandal begins with a very loaded line from Barbara, who offers advice to new teacher Sheba – 'Children are feral. Don't let them see your anxiety.' This line is ironic because it's actually Barbara who's feral and preys on Sheba's anxiety (about her affair with Steven). In fact, this line foreshadows the entire relationship that the film's plot will be based on – Barbara's animalistic manipulation of a 'wounded' Sheba.

At the start of *Mysterious Skin*, when we see Neil's first experience as a prostitute, the male client says to him: 'We're in Kansas, thank God. Not some big city full of diseases.' This is a key line in two ways. Firstly, it reinforces what will become Neil's narrative drive for the first half of the film – to get out of Hutchinson (Kansas). He soon feels stifled in the town and, although it's relatively safe and known, it's holding him back. And, of course, it's got all the memories of his time with the baseball coach. Secondly, the line foreshadows what'll become of Neil, and the life that he's going to start leading – having dangerous sexual experiences, leaving for New York City, and there finding himself in even more dangerous sexual situations.

Later in the film, in New York, Neil meets an AIDS victim during one of his escorting jobs. But the man doesn't want to have sex – he just wants to be touched. And so Neil rubs the man's back, as per his request. This gives him immense pleasure, the man repeatedly saying, 'Make me happy.' This is a key line because it reflects Neil's inner drive – to be happy, and wanted, and to feel special. Although at this point in the film it's not clear whether Neil knows this – he certainly doesn't express it – it's something we realise later, following his rape. It's here that he quickly realises – or at least overtly expresses – that what the coach did to him changed his life for ever. Having this line delivered by someone with AIDS, the very disease Neil's first client warned him of, neatly reminds us of both Neil's situation and one of the film's controlling ideas – finding happiness.

There's another key line in this film, delivered by Eric. When Brian and Eric get drunk on Brian's birthday, Eric jokes, 'I'm corrupting you… at last.' This is ironic because we've pretty much worked out by now that Brian's already been corrupted, sexually, by Neil and the coach. As well as being darkly ironic, this line sets up what Brian will himself learn shortly afterwards from Neil – that he has indeed been corrupted before. Structurally speaking, this is Brian's moment of reward – finally understanding what happened to him all those years before.

Nick, in *Nick and Norah's Infinite Playlist* (scr. Lorene Scafaria, 2008), says to his gay best friends, 'You guys don't know what it's like being straight. It's awful.' As well as providing obvious humour, a tongue-in-cheek prod at stereotypes of gay people being unhappy with themselves, this line summarises Nick's depression and what'll serve as the underlying drive for the whole film – his need to 'get over' his ex-girlfriend, Triss, and instead fall for 'good girl' Norah. Shortly after this line's delivered, in fact, Norah says to Triss right in front of Nick, 'There's no room for you, Triss. Not tonight.' This not only signals what'll develop later – Nick and Norah's romance – but nicely frames the story, which takes place over the course of just one night.

At the very end of the film, after all the fuss of trying to find The Little White Rabbits – which is the physical drive of the film – Nick and Norah decide to go home. And, because they've fallen for each other, they go home together, to get to know one another better. Because the whole film's been about them trying to find the band, though, Norah asks Nick if he's upset that they're missing the concert. Nick's reply is simple: 'We didn't miss it. This is it.' As well as providing a final punctuation mark to the screenplay – that their love was destined and now all will be all right – this line is key in that it represents the protagonists' abilities to shed their physical want (the band) and instead embrace their emotional need (each other). The line, therefore, feels important on a number of levels. It's one of those lines that you kind of knew was coming.

Whilst learning lines for an audition, Johnny in *In America* repeats, 'Why are we here? Why are we here?' As well as being credible –

these are the lines in the script he's learning – this is a key line summarising the situation he and his family are in. Essentially, they've moved from Ireland to America to try and get over the loss of their son, Frankie. So, when he says, 'Why are we here?' what he's really referring to is the premise of the film – the emotional journey that the family will go on as a result of moving to America.

Later, when wife Sarah is pregnant, she asks him to feel the baby kicking. He holds her stomach but tells her, 'I can't feel anything.' Again, as well as being entirely credible – he can't feel the baby kicking – what this line really refers to is the emotional void that he's found himself in following the death of their son, and how he desperately needs to grieve before it's too late and the family's destroyed. This idea's further clarified to the audience when he tells neighbour Mateo, 'I asked him [God] to take me instead of him [Frankie]. He took the both of us. And look what he put in my place… I'm a fucking ghost.'

In *Juno*, Vanessa says to Juno, 'A man becomes a father when he sees his baby.' Although she's saying this in defence of Mark, who's told her that he's not ready to be a father yet, the line acts as a set-up for the end of the film, where Bleeker – the biological father of Juno's baby – doesn't see his baby. Juno tells us in voiceover that she didn't want to see the baby, and nor did Bleeker. This is the raw truth of their situation – that they're not ready to be parents, and so can't see their baby. We see Vanessa hold what's now her baby, watched by Juno's stepmother Bren. Mark's nowhere in sight, having left Vanessa. This key line therefore also draws parallels between Mark and Bleeker – both are men who aren't ready to become a father – and so has the effect of pulling Vanessa and Juno together as mothers. By the end of the film, we feel that this has been Juno and Vanessa's story, and so Vanessa's line to Juno becomes even more key.

Before the birth, when Juno's worried that Vanessa and Mark splitting up might affect what happens to her baby, her father tells her that his best advice 'is to find someone who loves you for exactly what you are'. This key line works on two levels. Firstly, it clarifies Juno's decision to let Vanessa keep the baby, even without Mark there to help. She knows that all Vanessa wants is a baby, no matter whose it is and what it's like. She simply craves to be a mother. This line, then, confirms that Juno's made the right decision in letting Vanessa keep the baby. Secondly, this line also clarifies Juno's decision about her love for Bleeker. Throughout the film we've sensed that true love might emerge between the two, but Juno's always pushed it aside. We've also heard, on numerous occasions, that Bleeker likes everything about her – she's exactly what he wants. So, hearing this from her father propels Juno to accept the truth of the situation – that she and Bleeker love each other – and act upon it, leading to the film's resolution.

VOICEOVER

Many authors and teachers tell screenwriters to avoid voiceover. They see it as a way of cheating – of being lazy, and not striving for a way to cleverly convey what's happening in a character's mind. Voiceover can be cheating, it's true, but it can also be really sophisticated, and actually add something special to a screenplay. But only if it's considered carefully.

When we talk about voiceover, the assumption is that you just write what characters are thinking. That's why it's lazy – because it's a way of writing a character's internal thoughts rather than visualising them. But it's not really about that. Good voiceover doesn't just tell us what a character's thinking – it gives us a point of view about a situation, and complements the images that we're seeing on the screen. In this way, it's not about characters telling us what we can see – narrating the imagery – it's about characters giving us a way of understanding the images that we see. Good voiceover is written with perspective, letting us into the life of the character – perhaps their past – and not just hearing what they're saying about the here and now. Sometimes voiceover contradicts what we see on the screen, which tells us a lot about the character speaking. In this case, the voiceover works to give us a sense of who this person really is – of why they're seeing things differently to us.

Adaptation begins with a blank screen and Charlie's voiceover. It's an intense monologue telling us how he feels about himself. Through his constant self put-downs, we get a clear sense of his feelings of worthlessness and inability to connect with people – which is what the film goes on to explore. When the evolution montage comes in, Charlie's voiceover still running over the top if it, we're forced to make connections between what he's saying and what we're seeing. We know that he's a deep thinker and emotionalises everything.

American Beauty (scr. Alan Ball, 1999) starts with a voiceover from Lester, telling us what he thinks of his life. He talks directly to us about his feelings of loss and disconnection. Although we see some of the things that he's talking about – the slippers, his wife, his neighbours, etc – he's not just telling us what we're seeing. He's telling us about what we're seeing, adding a dramatic perspective to it. Again, this gives us a clear insight into his dramatic problem that goes on to drive the film.

In *Monster*, we see a montage of Aileen as a child, trying to enjoy her childhood but with it always being destroyed in some way – abuse, neglect, rejection, etc. Here, Aileen's voiceover is almost childlike, telling us about things that we perhaps recognise from our own childhood. This is a way of letting us empathise with her, challenging our perceptions about the crimes she commits. The voiceover comes back in strongly at the end of the film, too, reminding us that she never wanted to be how she turned out – she just wanted to be loved, like all of us. Her admission of defeat strikes a chord as we see her being taken away, eventually to be executed. It's a harrowing ending, emphasised by the formidable use of voiceover.

Having two voiceover narrators in *About a Boy* (scr. Peter Hedges, Chris Weitz & Paul Weitz, 2002) allows us to see the different perspectives about life that we'll see being explored in the film. Will is arrogant, deluded and happy being on his own, whilst Marcus is humble, realistic and desperate for friends. Through their opposing perspectives of life as told in voiceover, we know from the very start that these two characters are going to meet and learn something from each other. And, because we know what they're about – from the voiceover – we can take a pretty good guess what they will learn from each other.

Big Fish uses voiceover in a textured, sophisticated and highly engaging way. It's a film about storytelling – about people learning through stories and passing them on down the generations – so voiceover is entirely appropriate. From the very start, we learn through voiceover that the film's going to span many years and many perspectives. We hear three voices, two from Ed at different ages, and one from his son, Will. The voiceovers are interlaced with visual flashbacks to the stories being told, which, as well as being highly engaging – forcing us to work out what's going on and who's who – reinforce the idea of stories being passed down through the generations, each time having slightly different flavours. We learn by the end of the film that this is also a story about belief, so having a series of voiceovers that tells us these stories, in all their varieties, strengthens this theme. In this way, the use of voiceover in *Big Fish* isn't gimmicky or lazy – it's necessary.

As these examples show – and I'm sure you can think of many of your own – you shouldn't avoid using voiceover just because someone tells you it's bad. It can be clever, powerful and sometimes necessary. Where would *Notes on a Scandal* be without Barbara's voiceover, for example? What's important is that voiceover isn't just a way of relaying verbally what we can already see on the screen. It's about perspective point-of-view, and using it to deepen our understanding of character and story. It should be extremely well-crafted and peppered over visual imagery – not heavy and dominant, taking our attention away from what we're seeing at the same time.

Finally for this chapter, if you want to read more about dialogue then I recommend Rib Davis's book, *Writing Dialogue for Scripts* (2008). Most screenwriting books cover dialogue in some way, but this – as the title suggests – is a book purely about writing dialogue. It covers all areas of dialogue, from voice to subtext to voiceover. And remember – writing dialogue is hard. It's probably one of the hardest things about screenwriting. You need to keep honing and polishing and playing around with the words on the page. And, of course, you need to keep listening to the world and working out how and why people speak the way they do.

12. SELLING YOUR SCREENPLAY

So, you've written a great screenplay. It's got a cracking premise, a fantastic cast of characters, an original world, a brilliant narrative structure, dialogue that crackles and a visual landscape that makes the hairs on the back of your neck stand up. What next? How does this brilliant piece of work make it to the screen? Here's where the really hard work comes in – you have to try and sell your screenplay.

The first thing to remember about selling a screenplay is that there isn't only one way of doing it. You might have already sold your screenplay to the producer on the basis of a short outline or treatment. They loved the idea so much that they optioned it, meaning that they paid you a sum of money to hold onto the rights to the project for a period of time – six months, a year, five years, etc. Or, you might have made a pre-sale with a distributor who thought the idea was so strong that they felt they'd easily be able to sell it. They were impressed by the project's creative assets – the idea, the director or actor (if there are any attached), the soundtrack (if one's been created), even you as the writer. Or, you might have spent so long writing the screenplay that you know it better than you know your own life, meaning that when you go to pitch it to a producer or director they feel your passion and commission it straight away. Or maybe you're using a competition or funding scheme to get your screenplay read, and hoping that some kind of commission will follow.

However you approach trying to sell your screenplay – and you'll probably try many options at once – the key morsel of advice is that you've got to keep believing in your work and your ability to write, and not give up. But that's very easy to say. The going can get tough, without a doubt – piles of rejection letters, face-to-face refusals, negative feedback, etc – but, if you really want to make it, you have to persevere. And, of course, you have to think strategically. You have to try and turn threats into opportunities and weaknesses into strengths. You have to understand the market, learn the tricks of the trade – if, indeed, there are any – and be prepared to network like crazy. That said, you also have to know what you're talking about.

PITCHING DOCUMENTS

When trying to sell your screenplay, there are various documents that a buyer (or commissioner) might want to read. These are known as pitching documents, or selling documents. Basically, they serve two functions. First, they convey the story. This doesn't just mean letting the reader know what happens – though that's a major part of these documents – it means also giving a sense of the style and tone of the film, which includes the theme (how we should read the story). In other words, they should try and evoke a sense of feeling – as if the reader's experiencing the story as they work through the document. This is where good creative writing skills come in, using language to create the feel of the film. This might include vocabulary, syntax and the layout of words on the page.

Secondly, they should give a sense of the scale and logistics of the project, so that the reader can gauge how much the film would cost to make, and what kind of production logistics it'd require. This includes high-concept idea or not (will it appeal to the masses?), audience demographic (which might link to genre), cast size, locations and potential tie-ins (product placement, funding body schemes, music, actors, etc). Although discussions about some of this stuff would happen after someone expresses interest in optioning or commissioning your work, it's useful to try and give some sense of it at an early stage. If you think there's a particular benefit or selling point of your project – such as specific audience appeal or any talent already attached – then you should definitely write about it.

I talked about the purpose of development documents in Chapter 3 and, because pitching documents share many of the same qualities, I'll mention it again here. Whichever document you're working with, it should try and do the following:

- Capture the key structural elements (what happens?)
- Capture the key themes (what's it about?)
- Capture the imagination of the audience (why should I be interested?)
- Capture the style and tone of the film, and its intended audience (who's going to want to watch it?)

You need to know the essence of your screenplay – what it's about and why it should be made into a film – and you need to convey it well. Don't be satisfied with a first attempt at a pitching document – keep honing it so it's perfect. This might involve re-reading or thinking more about your screenplay, so that you really capture what it's about and appeal to the buyer or commissioner. This may very well be your one and only chance.

The first document you're likely to need – though it's actually not a document as such – is a **logline**. This is a short, sharp summary of all that the film is. It's usually only one sentence, though it can sometimes be two, and, in a snappy, clever and 'salesy' way, it needs to spell out who the protagonist is, the dramatic situation and/or world, what the protagonist's goal is – including their motivation – the main antagonism and the theme. Sometimes, too, the logline conveys a sense of the genre. The logline should give a sense of direction and dimensionality – in other words, not just the plot but also the theme. In other words, both the protagonist's physical and emotional journey. Don't confuse a logline with a tagline or strapline – that's something used specifically for advertising, like you'll see on a film's poster and/or DVD cover, and it's more of a hook than something that captures the story.

Here are some examples of possible loglines:

- *Ratatouille* – Remy, an oppressed rat living in Paris, follows his dream of being a famous cook by helping out a struggling young chef, and, although he almost jeopardises the restaurant and his own family in doing so, he manages to dispel people's prejudices towards the rat community.

- *Leap Year* – When uptight rich-bitch Anna follows her boyfriend to Ireland to propose to him, she finds herself thrown into a less-than-desirable road trip with the less-than-desirable Declan, only to be reminded of the true meaning of life and love.

- *Me and You and Everyone We Know* – Christine, a struggling video artist who has trouble connecting with people, finds herself pursuing divorced father-of-two Richard and, through her developing understanding of relationships, is able to produce a piece of video art that somebody wants to exhibit.

- *The Orphanage* (*El Orfanato*) (scr. Sergio G Sánchez, 2007) – When a young boy goes missing, his desperate mother does everything she can to find him, but, when she realises the awful truth of the situation, she has to make the biggest decision of her life – live without him or die and be with him.

An extension of the logline is the **synopsis**. This is a prose document that summarises the story, usually a page in length. A synopsis can be more neutral and matter-of-fact than longer documents, though I'd always encourage you to add dramatic flavour where you can. A synopsis might use the logline first – as a title, perhaps – followed usually by three paragraphs. Paragraph one sets up the story and the situation – Act 1; paragraph two develops the story and details the complications/hurdles – Act 2; and paragraph three gives the resolution of the story, with its emotional punctuation mark – Act 3. It's important to hit the key beats of the story here, and not give too much detail about things that are less important, as it's the document that might make or break your potential deal – the 'bite' that will make them want to read more (outline, treatment, etc).

A longer and more detailed version of the synopsis is the **outline**. Still a relatively short document in the grand scheme of things – usually two to three pages – it tells the story in its entirety. It can flesh out the key beats more than the synopsis, and better bring out the intended emotion. Secondary characters might be introduced in the outline, too, helping to map the bigger landscape of the narrative. It's usually written in polished, powerful prose – creative writing! – denoting the relevant feeling and tone of the film. The style of writing in the outline can reflect the writer's voice, which again might link with the feeling and tone of the story.

I've already discussed the **treatment** in Chapter 3, so go back and remind yourself of this document. It's often one of the most important documents used for selling a feature film because of the detail it goes into. In a way, it's just one step short of reading the screenplay – apart from dialogue and visual texture, it lays out all of the action and emotion.

Creative exercise
Try writing a logline for a screenplay that you're working on. When you're happy with it, see if you can develop it into a synopsis. Then, try to extend that into an outline. Some people find it easier to work backwards – starting big and then boiling down to find the essence – so do it that way if you prefer. If you can, test the documents out on a fellow screenwriter.

THINKING STRATEGICALLY

It sounds obvious, but you really do have to be strategic when you're trying to sell your screenplay. What I mean by this, quite simply, is that you need to think carefully about what you're doing and work out a strategy for how you're going to achieve your goal. For example, it's no good sending a children's film to a literary agency that doesn't deal with children's films. Or, it's no good submitting a feature film idea to a competition that's aimed at television series. This sounds really obvious, I know, but it's surprising how many people seem to be oblivious of, or else ignore, such things. Not only is it a waste of time and effort, it could paint you in a bad light – and people in the industry, whether they're agents, producers, directors or readers, talk – a lot.

The first thing to consider is how you're going to get your script into the right hands – the producer's, the director's, the actor's, etc. Depending on the kind of project you're working on, and whether you're looking to sustain a career as a screenwriter or just try and make films yourself, one of the first questions you might ask yourself is whether or not you need an agent or manager. Historically, most screenwriters have had agents or managers – someone who's represented their creative projects and found them work through their expansive contacts and relentless networking. There's no denying that an agent can do a lot for your career – find you work, negotiate your contracts, keep you sane, etc – and having one can certainly make you feel good, and like you're a real writer. They might take their ten or fifteen per cent commission, but it's worth it because of everything they do for you. Nowadays, however, people are relying less and less on agents. Because we're all able to find our own networks – especially through social media websites such as Facebook, Twitter and LinkedIn – the idea that we need someone to put us in touch with people and recommend our work is becoming outdated. There are so many avenues for 'getting in touch with' and 'following' the right people these days that many emerging screenwriters aren't consciously looking for agents or managers. 'Real' networking events such as screenwriting festivals and conferences allow screenwriters and producers to meet, talk and pitch ideas – whether formally, such as a speed pitching session, or informally, such as over drinks in the bar. Therefore, is the agent needed? It's a good question – and only you'll know the path you want to take – though there are two quite specific reasons why an agent might be a good choice. First of all, many production companies and broadcasters won't look at work unless it's sent to them by an agent. Second, if you're lucky enough to get a commission, an agent will know exactly what to look for in the contract that will benefit you both creatively and financially. So if you really haven't got eyes for small print or a head for figures, an agent could be a good bet.

If you are thinking about approaching an agent, here are some tips:

- Do your homework and find out about the agents you're approaching. Look at what kind of work – and writers – they deal with, and ask yourself whether or not you fit the bill.

- Don't be afraid to send your work to a few agents simultaneously. People often hear stories that you should only send work to one agent at a time – but with the success rate quite slim, why waste time by waiting weeks or months to hear from your only shot?

- Find out whether they prefer paper or e-mailed copies of work. Some agents will ask for e-mailed work – in which case you'd better make sure you send it in a format they can open – whereas some will ask for it to be sent in the post, to save their costs. Respect their preferences – don't be cheap if they ask for a paper copy!

- Don't give up, especially if they seem interested in your work. It took three screenplays before my first agent took me on.

The first he liked, but wanted to see what else I had – i.e., was I committed, or just trying my luck? The second he didn't like very much at all, though he could see my potential as a screenwriter. The third he liked a lot, and thought he might be able to sell it. We did get it optioned, though it never got made. But the point is this – if I hadn't persevered, and proven myself as a committed screenwriter with career ambitions, he wouldn't have taken me on.

- If you're lucky enough to have a meeting before you're taken on, go with a few ideas and some samples of your work. Have something to talk about, too – the films you like, the experiences you've had, the ambitions you hold, the people you know who might be able to help you get something made, etc.

- If you do get an agent – well done – don't think that everything will just fall into place. You've still got to work hard and network yourself. Continue to find competitions, pitching events, etc, to prove your worth. Use your agent to help you when you're getting somewhere, not just to get you all the meetings in the first place.

If you're planning to go it alone then you definitely have to think and act more strategically. You have to take on the role of the agent yourself, not just the eager screenwriter. For example, it's no good just having a great product – many people have that. You need to know how you're going to turn that product into something that's going to get made, or at least optioned. That's why you need to be market savvy and keep on top of things – trends, tastes, movements, productions, competitions, funding schemes, etc. You also have to be somewhat ruthless, which doesn't mean being nasty or willing to shaft your mates, but involves being forward thinking and prepared to make sacrifices in order to achieve your goals. This might manifest itself in a variety of ways, from working evenings and weekends to get the right pitching documents together, to travelling up and down the country to attend networking events and festivals, to spending money on training that will help you understand laws, policies, grant writing, etc. Some people thrive on this and are very good at it. Others shy away and don't want to understand – in which case they will most definitely need an agent!

From writing your screenplay and putting together a range of pitching documents (as above), you should have a strong idea about where your project might sit. This could mean commercially – as in, what's a film production company looking for at the minute and does yours have the potential to hit the spot? – but it could also mean creatively – as in, what script development schemes are currently 'recruiting' writers and projects, and does yours have something in it that they're looking for (location, theme, genre, etc)? Whichever opportunities exist out there, it's your job to evaluate them and see, where possible, if you can tailor your project accordingly. Sometimes people are looking for screenplays set in particular worlds. Sometimes they're looking for screenplays in a specific genre. And sometimes they're looking for writers of a particular background, who can tell a certain kind of story related to an event, person, theme, context, etc. Obviously your screenplay's not going to fit all of these opportunities, but sometimes it pays to think carefully about how you can package it to at least get past the first hurdle. In this sense, you're not just a screenwriter but also someone who knows the bottom line.

INDUSTRY INSIGHT

Sandra Cain is an author, writer and lecturer, specialising in creative writing, publishing and public relations. Her books include *Key Concepts in Public Relations* (2009) and *Media Writing: A Practical Introduction* (2010). She has this to say:

Marketing your screenplay

A screenplay is a product – and, as such, should be marketed and sold like all other products. The whole point of a successful marketing campaign is to sell a service or a tangible asset at a profit. The Chartered Institute of Marketing defines marketing as 'the management process responsible for identifying, anticipating and satisfying customer requirements profitably'. The American Marketing Association defines marketing rather more precisely in describing it as 'the process of planning and executing the conception, pricing and distribution of ideas, goods and services to create exchanges that satisfy individual and organisational objectives'.

'But hey,' I hear you say, 'this is a screenplay, not a tin of Boston Beans!' That doesn't matter – the fundamentals of marketing still need to be considered. A good place to start is with what marketers call the **Four Ps – Product, Price, Place** (Distribution) and **Promotion**. In the case of the screenplay, the product is the physical screenplay itself – the tangible creative output you want to get made as a film, to be viewed by a global audience. Pricing takes into account any profit margins set in place by the production company. Place is associated with channels of distribution – who's going to see the movie, where, and how. Finally, promotion – the decisions related to communicating and selling the film to potential audiences.

In the case of selling the screenplay, there are two avenues. The first is to sell to a production company, who'll option the screenplay and hopefully one day make the film. The second is to try and sell directly to the market – crowd sourcing, private investment, etc. This might fund you to get the film made yourself.

Many production companies nowadays only accept screenplay submissions from people they know and trust – agents, established producers, entertainment solicitors and writers with a track record. It can be really hard to get someone to read your script when you don't have an agent – though it's not impossible. If you're an independent filmmaker then the ball's in your court. And this is when marketing your screenplay really kicks in. Without the backing of a production company, you're pretty much on your own – and this is where the Boston Beans come in.

You'll need to plan your marketing programme as you would a military campaign. It can't be an ad-hoc affair – it must be sustained and tactical. You'll need to ask yourself the following questions:

- What should the marketing plan achieve? (What are the plan's objectives?)

- Who should the plan talk to? (Who's my audience?)

- What does the plan want to say? (What are the messages the plan should communicate?)

- How should the plan say it? (Which marketing tools and techniques should the plan use to relay the right messages?)

- Has the plan worked? (What are the measures of success?)

Your marketing plan should be a tactical document based on in-depth research that outlines the strategy and initiatives. The five major stages of planning are:

1. Analysis of the market
2. Marketing objectives
3. Audience and demographics
4. Messages
5. Timescales

You'll need to consider the marketing tools and techniques you'll use to persuade your potential audiences and buyers (in the case of merchandising) to come to market and part with their money. These tactics are important tools of influence, and are an important part of the marketing campaign. Remember, tactics have weaknesses as well as strengths, and an efficacious marketing programme should select a range of techniques that complement each other and, when taken together, offer a potent set of messages. Be sure to include traditional marketing techniques as well as online, digital, guerrilla and social media.

© Sandra Cain, 2012

FINDING FUNDING

As I've already mentioned, there are numerous funding schemes out there that are geared towards screenwriters working on feature films. National and regional screen bodies and arts organisations have a duty to develop talent and spend a portion of their budget on screenplay development, which you should investigate and try to tap into. Although such schemes vary from country to country and even from region to region, they all share the same function – to develop local writing talent and create films that are commercially and culturally successful – and may manifest themselves in one of the following ways:

- **Training** – you might be funded to attend screenplay training courses, development hothouses, masterclasses, etc, to help raise the quality of your screenplay.

- **Research** – you might be funded to undertake research that will help you complete a screenplay, such as travelling to interview key people or accessing archives for primary materials.

- **Networking** – you might be funded to attend a screenwriting festival or conference, or similar networking event, to boost the chances of your screenplay being commissioned.

- **Mentoring** – probably the most common type of screenplay development funding, you might be funded to work with a script editor, development executive or producer to generate further – better – drafts of your screenplay, ready to offer to the marketplace.

If you're keen to get your film made regardless of production companies and broadcasters, and especially if you're a writer-director, then you might consider crowd funding as a way of earning enough money to turn your screenplay into an actual film. Although it's a relatively new concept, it works on the basis of some of the principles used in traditional film financing – namely, that those with a vested interest in having a film made and putting good stories out there will donate money. Although much crowd funding is done 'in kind', perhaps from family and friends, some of it's in recognition of things like product placement and credit (associate producer, executive producer) – so not at all dissimilar to traditional film financing.

Like self-publishing, films made through crowd funding might be viewed as negative. People may see them as 'vanity films' or not 'real' films. Although it's clear where this view comes from, it's not really true. At the end of the day, it's a legitimate way to get a film made – a film that's been written with passion – and although it's not been funded traditionally, that doesn't mean that it's of a lesser quality. Such films are often made for other reasons, too, such as to showcase the writer and/or director's work, which might lead to other, 'proper' projects – or to prove that a controversial story can be told effectively, which, once this has been recognised via audience and industry reactions, might be picked up by a distributor anyway, and turned back into a 'proper' project.

Popular crowd funding websites include Indiegogo, Kickstarter and PleaseFundUs. As with most things these days, it's not good enough to just have a product and an opportunity – you need to have a solid communications strategy, which undoubtedly means using social media. If you've got a great screenplay that you want to get made, and the way of getting it made is through a crowd funding website, then you clearly have to drive traffic to that website. If you want the bucks, you have to get the looks! So, for example, you might think about setting up a website for the project, which could very easily be a Facebook or Wordpress page – where there's a format and design tools already in place, and you simply have to fill it with relevant content and style. This could be complemented by a Twitter account, which you can use to send out project updates and other related newsfeeds. Once you've captured an audience – a Facebook 'like' that's there to stay, and a Twitter 'follower' who's always going to get your updates – you can start to create a virtual community that will hopefully help you both financially and promotionally, such as telling others about the film project.

Although crowd funding can open the floodgates to a project being realised, there are also things you need to be careful about. For example, what are the funders getting from the project? What can you promise them – and what can you not? Do you have different levels of funding in place, with associated credits, and, if so, what happens if you get many more or many fewer than you anticipated? There are also practical things to consider, such as whose bank account will the money go into – the company's or yours – and who's going to manage the Facebook and Twitter accounts – especially if they attract dozens of hits a day? This is where getting a producer on board really helps. Their role is generally much more concerned with project management – budgets, schedules, contracts, etc – which, as a creative, you might really need to have in the mix.

There are many facets to a crowd funded film, then, which you may or may not want to get involved in. If you do, then there are clearly great opportunities for your film to be made, giving you that elusive credit as well as the satisfaction of seeing your screenplay on the screen. And, of course, there are hundreds of well-respected film festivals around the world that might screen your film, which could lead to other opportunities. If you're definitely interested in this type of venture, Spanner Films has compiled a comprehensive guide to crowd funding, which you should look up online.

13. SELLING YOURSELF AS A SCREENWRITER

An important – though often unwritten about – aspect of being a screenwriter is how to sell yourself. Yes, it's important to know how to sell your work, but it's also important to consider how you can sell yourself as a screenwriter – your voice, your ideas, your ability to undertake a commission, etc. Sometimes you might be asked about your work, and why you should be given the opportunity to have your screenplay developed. In other words, why you? There might be specific reasons why you need to tell this story – such as personal experience or the fact that you've got contacts who'll help the film see the light of day – or it might simply be a case of you trying to prove that you're a writer with a burning ambition to tell this story, with the passion and dedication that will see the screenplay through numerous drafts and lots of ups and downs.

At other times, you'll be specifically asked to draw on your sense of self because you're looking to be hired to write or re-write a screenplay. This notion of 'screenwriter for hire' is little understood outside the field, but, as you might already know, it's a big part of the screenwriter's life. Ideally, we'll all write our own films that will be made and receive critical and financial success. But the reality is that this is only a small part of the screenwriting market. It's likely throughout your career as a screenwriter that you'll be taken on to write someone else's idea – a producer or actor, for example – or you'll be brought in to re-write someone else's screenplay – after which someone might be brought in to re-write your version. Although some screenwriters might not see this as an ideal situation, it's certainly one that pays – which is important! – and it's also one that helps to build credits and profile. Also, a writer who's been commissioned to write someone else's screenplay, perhaps on the strength of their own work, can then be recommended to write someone else's, and then someone else's after that. And, hopefully, at some point, someone's going to ask what original ideas they have – their own screenplays.

This is where the notion of the **calling-card** script comes into play. Essentially, this is one or more screenplays that the screenwriter is proud of, and that best shows their writing talent. Although it might be touted around the industry to try and get a commission, it can also act as a really solid calling-card for other work – writers and re-writers for hire. For example, a producer looking to commission a writer might be seeking someone who can write really strong female characters, or who's got a knack for satire. This is where the calling-card script comes in. Or, a producer might be looking for someone to re-write a screenplay that's structurally not very sound, and so is seeking someone who knows how to use structure well. Again, this is where the calling-card script comes in. A producer, director, actor or anyone looking to hire a screenwriter could be looking for any one thing at any time, which is why it's important to have work that shows off your abilities. Whether you're an expert in a particular genre, brilliant at writing minor characters, or have a gift for writing razor-sharp dialogue, your calling-card work should demonstrate this well because you never know where it might lead.

CAREER PLANNING

Although the industry moves very fast, and people's roles, tastes and working practices change daily, it's still essential to have at least some idea of where you want to be, and how you want to get there. And, of course, where you've come from, and what you can learn from that.

Without some sense of strategy, you might find yourself grabbing at every opportunity and getting none. Or, alternatively, running around in so many directions that you become lost and unfocused.

Your specific sense of career planning will undoubtedly relate to your experiences, ambitions and opportunities, but here are some examples of positions you might find yourself in:

- **You're a brand new screenwriter and don't have any industry contacts. What do you do?** Well, building networks is a good start. Look out for local film or writing festivals and try to meet people. Start reading the industry press, too, and keep an eye out for bigger networking events, competitions and funding schemes.

- **You've been short-listed for various competitions, and someone's been interested in your work, but nothing's come of it.** This is a good starting point to think about approaching agents or managers. Your competition successes show your enthusiasm as well as your talent, and an agent or manager is likely to be looking for someone who's going to work hard themselves. Having someone interested in your work is also a good launch pad for the agent or manager to get involved – setting up further meetings, talking business, etc.

- **You've had a few short films made, and they've been screened internationally, and now you want to try and get a feature off the ground. You've got contacts but aren't sure about their feature film experiences.** Again, this is a good starting point. The fact that you've had things made puts you in a different position when it comes to collaboration and funding opportunities. You've got a showreel, which helps a lot – it moves from words on a page to words and images on a screen. If you're pitching your feature idea, have your short films on hand to show people how your ideas translate to the screen. And look out for funding opportunities that are aimed at those with some experience already. Sometimes these funding schemes try to put creative teams together – screenwriter, director, etc.

- **You've had a feature film made, which was screened at various international film festivals, but it was made on a very low budget that mainly came through crowd funding.** This is another really great platform from which to try and get further work. The fact that it's a feature tells us a lot – that you can sustain a story that long, that you can work with a big creative team over a period of time, that you've shown determination to get the screenplay realised, etc. A feature like this might open doors for being hired to write or re-write another screenplay, which could pay well. This will give you further credits and profile, which could lead to other work, and so on.

- **You've been hired to write many screenplays for other people's ideas, and you've even been brought on to re-write a couple of other screenplays. Some have been made and some haven't. You're desperate to get your own film idea made.** The fact that you've been hired numerous times tells us something about your screenwriting abilities, which is a great thing. It puts you in a strong position regarding funding and development schemes because you've got a track record – and, importantly, you're on the edge of moving into a new realm. If you're still treading water then maybe a low-budget feature is the way to go. It shouldn't dampen your profile in any way because you've already got a track record of being hired and being produced.

Do any of these situations sound like you? Or where you'd like to be in a number of years' time? If so, then consider them carefully and look around for possible opportunities that you might want to take advantage of, either now or further down the line.

INDUSTRY INSIGHT

Dr Helen Jacey, screenwriter, lecturer and author of *The Woman in the Story: Writing Memorable Female Characters* (2010), has this to say:

The SWOT analysis for screenwriters

As screenwriters embarking on creative careers, we don't often see ourselves needing business management knowledge, let alone entrepreneurial skills. But these skills, essential to the growth and success of all businesses, are in many ways just as relevant to the career path of the creative freelancer. Our job can be relatively isolated and reactive without obvious ways of keeping on track. There are many ways of stepping back and seeing the big picture. A useful one is the SWOT analysis. Tried and tested in the business world, it can be a surprisingly effective model for planning and developing both your creative projects and longer-term career plans.

Very simply, the SWOT analysis stands for **Strengths**, **Weaknesses**, **Opportunities** and **Threats**. Through a brainstorming exercise, you can consider these factors in dealing with dilemmas such as 'what project next?' or 'how to buy more time to write?'

This is what a SWOT analysis can look like:

Let's apply it to the challenge of building a successful career as a screenwriter. Remember, this is a completely individual exercise as everyone is unique, with completely different circumstances. The results also will change over time, as your career grows.

Strengths

Think about all the obvious – and not so obvious – skills, talents, support systems and general 'advantageous' factors in your possession. Some of these you might completely take for granted, like hidden gems. Think of your strengths as a treasure trove of resources – even those you don't realise are buried beneath your feet!

For screenwriters, these can be your imagination, your tenacity, your passion for film and television, your love of story, your love of people. It can be freedom to write, family support, a special place for your creativity where you can have peace and quiet. It can be your supportive agent, your networking abilities, your emerging track record.

Ask yourself:

- What are my achievements, and which of my personal qualities have made these possible?
- What resources do I have to write?
- What support systems do I trust and value?

Weaknesses

Conventional wisdom tells us that a small problem can turn into a crisis if ignored. Conversely, we're also told to look on the bright side and not to dwell on the negative! Confusing... A more helpful way of thinking about your weaknesses in terms of your career is to honestly appraise 'areas for improvement'. This is a solution-focused way of looking at those issues that could be lurking beneath the surface.

For screenwriters, weaknesses can be a lack of track record, lack of connections, a lack of agent, a lack of support systems. It could be a lack of choosing the right project. You might have a day job that drains all your energy. Personal weaknesses can be anything from severe introversion, a hatred of networking, missing deadlines, and sloppy punctuation.

Ask yourself:

- Do I have enough creative ideas? Do I have self-discipline to see them through?
- Do I have confidence and self-belief?
- Do I have support from others – emotionally, materially, or any other way important to my success?
- Do I understand how people see me, and what people might find difficult about working with me?

Opportunities

As freelancers, it's all too easy to react to external opportunities rather than creating our own. Ideally, you'll have a working life made up of both. While the 'paid gig' is more than welcome, becoming the 'jobbing hack' can foster cynicism and be a real creativity killer. Creating your own opportunities will make you feel more in control of your creative and economic destiny, and can also result in more entrepreneurial benefits, such as higher profit participation and more ownership in your ideas. While William Goldman reminds us 'nobody likes to say yes first', by originating your story and getting it to the screen – perhaps by becoming a writer-producer – you're saying 'yes' first.

Ask yourself:

- Am I a good networker? Do I go to enough events?
- Am I promoting my ideas?

- Am I aware of local and regional film initiatives? Do I respond quickly to opportunities?
- Am I doing my homework on what's out there? Am I 'out there'?

Threats

There's no doubt life can be turbulent for the budding writer. 'Know Thy Enemy' is a good principle that can help you plan for the unexpected, like imagination or money drying up, rival projects going into production before yours has evolved from treatment into a draft, or feeling let down by people you're working with. 'What if...' is a good way of appraising the more challenging risks in your career.

Ask yourself:

- How would I handle things going wrong?
- What strengths would I utilise to resolve or minimise threats?
- Which of my weaknesses might have contributed to these happening?
- How can I turn a threat into an opportunity?

© Helen Jacey, 2012

Once you start to think about yourself in these ways, it's surprising what you'll realise about yourself and your work. You might never have thought about doing this – reflecting on who you are and planning how to make successes out of shortcomings – but it's so useful. It's only when you take a step back and look at the bigger picture – your life, your talents, the film industry, etc – that you understand how you fit into it all – your past, present and future. If you're a student of screenwriting, this is something you might be asked to think about regularly, as part of your coursework. Your lecturers want you to do well – hopefully! – and want you to be a shining beacon example of success. Even if you're not a student, thinking of your place in the market – the very tough and very saturated market – and how you might want to make your mark, is both enlightening and productive.

INDUSTRY INSIGHT

Former Disney executive Kathie Fong Yoneda, the author of *The Script-Selling Game: A Hollywood Insider's Look At Getting Your Script Sold and Produced* (2011), who consults with clients across the world, has this to say:

Who are you, and what makes you different?
Knowing who you are and what makes you different will go a long way when it comes to moving you out into the professional world. Since there are thousands of college graduates eager to get jobs in the entertainment industry, you have to establish an identity. One common tactic used in the US is to have your own logline – an interesting two or three sentences that gives others a sense of who you are and where you're headed.

Example 1 – *'I'm a grad student in cinematography at USC and eventually want to work in television. On weekends, I work at an electronic chain store as a sales rep and started a series of 'how to' workshops for customers who've just bought new digital equipment and want to make home movies. The corporate office liked the series so much they're featuring it on their website.'*

Why this works – This clearly shows us this grad student is a self-starter and managed to integrate her future career path into her part-time job.

<u>Example 2</u> – *'I'm in my last year of undergrad in film studies and started working as an intern for a literary agency. I guess my barista skills at Starbucks have really paid off because, in between making lattes for my bosses, they're now having me read and evaluate submissions for some of their clients.'*

Why this works – This demonstrates the student isn't afraid to start at the bottom, and put his past experience to good use. Having a part-time job or interning while attending college also makes us aware that this student is good at multi-tasking.

Even if you're just coming out of college and you haven't had much business experience, think of what you have to offer that others might value, which, in turn, will have them remember you and want to make time for you. Can you speak another language? Did you do any studying abroad? Are you a major foodie? Do you have an unusual hobby?

The bottom line – When making the transition from college to working professional, it's important to establish realistic goals – realistic means goals that are do-able. There are goals and there are dreams. Both are good to aspire to, but you have to look at the big picture. Getting a job in the industry (any job) is getting your foot in the door. Goals should be established to help you move your way forward and upward.

The film studies student I mentioned was an intern, working for free. His job had him being a 'go-for'. He didn't complain, he did his job well and he was rewarded when they trusted him enough to start reading and evaluating material for some of their clients. He realised that gaining greater responsibility was a realistic goal. Becoming an agent in one or even six months isn't a realistic goal.

© Kathie Fong Yoneda, 2012

PROMOTING YOURSELF AS A SCREENWRITER

To take these ideas one step further, when you're starting to develop your screenwriting career – or even when in the thick of it, when you're starting to get recognition for your work – you might want to think more specifically about how you promote or market yourself as a screenwriter. You might know who you are, what you stand for, and what you aim to achieve – but how do you get that across to others? How might thinking about yourself as a brand help you to show the world who you are as a screenwriter, and – ultimately – help you to garner more success?

Screenwriting agent Julian Friedmann believes this is becoming much more of a concern for the contemporary screenwriter. In an article for *MovieScope Magazine*, he estimated the biggest change over the last decade is how screenwriters spend their professional time – namely, that less time is spent on writing and more time is spent on marketing themselves. This is especially true with the rise of social media – many screenwriters today have websites, blogs, and Facebook, Twitter and LinkedIn accounts – but it also includes attending networking events organised by the industry, where screenwriters get to schmooze, swap cards and pitch their ideas at any given opportunity.

Although, on the face of it, it might sound like a crass intervention, thinking strategically about how you promote or market yourself as a screenwriter could bring you great rewards. For example, you might be the screenwriter with the acid tongue – the one who writes killer lines that has an audience gagging for more. And if someone's looking to hire a writer with such skills, it might be you. Or you might be the screenwriter who's overcome the hardest of odds to achieve what you have, giving people a strong sense that these films have been written by a real person with real guts and tenacity. Although we could argue that this might have no bearing on the story, when it comes to the industry and selling a film to audiences, it's something very tangible that will ultimately affect how many people are interested in it. On the other hand, this kind of thing might impact the screenplay in noticeable ways – it might give your writing a certain 'edge' or feeling, bestowing identifiable hallmarks on your work.

INDUSTRY INSIGHT

Sandra Cain has this to say:

Marketing yourself as a screenwriter

To sell is to brand. A screenplay can be branded in its entirety, or form part of a branded empire. A non-fiction book can be branded. A novel can be branded. A magazine can be branded. And you, the screenwriter, can also be branded.

Simply put, a brand is a name, term, design or symbol that identifies and differentiates products. In reality, a brand is much more than this – it speaks of values and associations. Brand associations are what a brand means to a customer in terms of what they automatically – and unconsciously – think about the product or service. Brand values speak of concepts such as tradition, excitement, provocation and nostalgia. So how can you apply these principles to yourself, as a real-life writing human being?

When you think of screenwriters like Nora Ephron, Jason Segal and Charlie Kaufman, you know what you're going to get. When you think of fiction writers like Stephen King, Chuck Palahniuk and Toni Morrison, you also know what you're going to get. But 'knowing what you're going to get' goes beyond ideas of the product's genre. It's more about sustainable values, image and backstory.

Every writer has a story – their written one and their personal one. Some writers choose to share their personal story – it becomes part of their brand. Think, for example, of Diablo Cody, the writer of *Juno*, and JK Rowling, writer of the *Harry Potter* series. Here we have similar personal stories – a pole dancer and blogger, using whatever means she could to earn a living, and a single parent writing in a café, nursing a cup of cold coffee to save money on the heating bills in her tiny council flat. With both writers, think how their stories have changed since becoming hugely successful.

As a screenwriter, it's well worth considering your public persona – your brand image – and using it as a marketing tool. It'll become a generally accepted concept for what you are and stand for, and will incorporate all the visual, verbal and behavioural elements that make up 'you'. It matters what you say, what you do, and what others say and think about you. Your image should spark interest in your audience – it should speak to them. It should stand for good value, recognition and consistency. Only when you're sure of your image can you then begin to think about the tools and techniques you'll use to market yourself as that screenwriter.

© Sandra Cain, 2012

Whatever is intrinsically you, and however you might be able to brand yourself, spend time thinking about it and assessing its potential. Audiences don't necessarily want you to lay on a self-proclaimed story for the sake of it – that could be very off-putting – but if there's a way to use elements of your life and your experiences to help promote you as the writer of your work, then why not? After all, you are a storyteller.

14. SURVIVING AS A SCREENWRITER

There are two key elements to surviving as a screenwriter – literally surviving in the marketplace (work and money), and also surviving as a creative, sustaining and retaining your talent and voice. It's clearly very important to earn money and be able to live, and it's important to build your profile and list of credits. As discussed in Chapter 13, these two facets can be interlinked, such as being paid to write screenplays for other people's ideas, or being paid to re-write an existing screenplay. Whereas some people might see this as selling your soul, most sensible people will view it as being realistic, productive – and usefully strategic. At the same time, however, it's also important to remain true to yourself and the writing you want to produce. If you spend too long writing for other people, or change your work too many times because of the notes you receive, you might find that you lose faith in both the industry and your creative abilities as a screenwriter.

But how do you start, and how do you know when to stop? And what happens when you're given an opportunity that's too good to miss, but which will take you away from your own – or favourite – project? Only you can know the answer to this, of course, but it's worth stepping back every so often and reflecting on where you are and where you want to be – see the SWOT analysis in Chapter 12, for example – so that you don't lose sight of your aims, ambitions and abilities. This isn't meant to be all 'touchy feely', but a reality check about what you're doing. Sometimes you really need to get a story out, and so will have to sacrifice other work in favour of telling the story that's driving you. At other times you might have a personal project you're chipping away at happily, but, because you need a new car or a new roof on your house, have to take on a commission in order to pay for it. Life is never simple, as we all know, and elements like these are all part of the joy and the pain of surviving as a screenwriter.

FIRST STEPS

Whether you're new to screenwriting or have a lot of experience already, there are always first steps that need to be taken. For a new screenwriter, first steps might include getting to know how the industry works, getting to know people, understanding a contract and having the confidence to respond to people's notes on your screenplay. For an experienced screenwriter, first steps might be getting to know a new producer, working out how you fit into a new project that you've been hired on to, understanding how storytelling works on a new platform that you're working on, or understanding the cultural differences of a contract. Although there might be marked differences between new and experienced screenwriters, in the end we're all in it together. We're all here to tell good stories and make successful films – and one minute you might be making it, and the next you might not. If there's one rule in screenwriting that applies to everyone, it's that success is never guaranteed and, just because you've made something once, it doesn't mean you're going to make it again. As people often say, you're only as good as your last screenplay.

INDUSTRY INSIGHT

Kathie Fong Yoneda has this to say:

The value of volunteering and interning
By and large, in this present-day economy, jobs won't auto-matically come to you. But showing your passion and abilities

to others is as easy as doing volunteer work or working as an intern.

Example 1 – *'Starting out in the industry, I was a receptionist for the legal department at a major studio. The President of the Motion Picture division asked if I had time after work to stuff envelopes for a special event he was chairing. Out of curiosity, I looked at the invitation and realised it was a fundraiser for breast cancer research. I checked the date of the event, which happened to be a free day for me. I asked if he needed any help the day of the fundraiser and it turned out he needed more volunteers to man the silent auction tables. I quickly recruited a few of my friends, who also worked in film/TV, to help out. When a job opened up as an assistant for a new senior VP in motion pictures, the big boss called me on the intercom and said he'd like to give me a personal recommendation for the job, which I got! In addition, I referred one of my friends I recruited for the charity event and she got my old job!'*

Why this worked – Volunteers might not get paid in money. But for those volunteers who show exceptional skills and are willing to extend themselves, it can pay off further down the road. In this case, it not only paid off for the person concerned, but for one of their colleagues.

Example 2 – *'While interning at a network, one proactive intern enthusiastically volunteered to spend a few hours a week updating the website of a new network TV show. Every day, the intern would diligently read the comments and questions from fans. With the permission of the show-runner and the network, the intern started a discussion group. He would post an intriguing question or topic each day that had to do with either a key storyline or an important character of the show. In a few short weeks, traffic on the show's website had jumped three-fold. He realised many of the responders were female and seemed to be taking quite an interest in one of the secondary male characters. Noting this, the intern talked to the supervising producer and suggested that a blog be written once a week from the point of view of that particular male character, and he volunteered to write the blog.*

As a result of the large number of hits and the response to the intern's blog, the network quickly recognised the popularity of that character and that he deserved more exposure. The enterprising intern gave the show-runner and supervising producer an episodic premise he'd written which, coincidentally, prominently featured the character, and he was allowed to write the episode under the watchful eye of one of the story editors. As the series started featuring that character more often, the Nielsen ratings, likewise, started to rise. None of this would've happened if the intern hadn't used the show's website to increase interest in the series – which is where he's now happily working on the writing staff.'

Why this worked – This intern definitely showed his 'creative' spirit as well as a solid work ethic. You'll notice he took his time and waited until he'd proven his worth before making his move and asking if the show-runner and supervising producer would be willing to look at an episodic premise he'd written, featuring the on-the-rise secondary character. He clearly recognised how important it was to prove himself first, and then build a relationship before requesting a favour.

The bottom line – The most successful networking means putting yourself out there and showing others what you can do – even if you aren't getting paid. Just because you have a degree in film studies doesn't mean you have the experience to immediately become an executive at a studio, or to write or produce a TV series. Building relationships while showcasing your abilities will usually pay off in the long run, if you play your cards right.

© Kathie Fong Yoneda, 2012

JOINING FORCES

The value of networking has been flagged up numerous times in this book, mainly to do with the business side of screenwriting and finding ways of selling your work. Another side to this is the personal value that networking can give you – moral support, inspiration, a feeling of connectedness, etc. Screenwriting can, on the whole, be a lonely process – at least until you sell your work and start to have input from a myriad of people. Until then, though, it can literally be a case of you, your laptop and a room. Although you need the creative space to perform, you also need support networks and places you can interact with like-minded people.

One way this can be achieved is by joining, or setting up, a writers' group. Meeting with other screenwriters on a regular basis – once a week, once a month, etc – not only gives you moral support and people to discuss current issues with; it gives you a structure within which to develop your work. For example, you might have to produce a piece to be workshopped at the next meeting, or you might have to read and comment on someone else's work. Although, on occasions, you might feel like this is taking you away from your screenplay, it can actually be really beneficial. This isn't just because it helps to get feedback on your own stuff; it's also a way of making you step away from your work periodically to connect with other people who can help you work through issues – craft problems, industry developments, personal dilemmas, etc. You might even find someone that you'd like to try and co-write a screenplay with, which, as well as being an interesting experiment for you both, is another way of helping to structure your working life and keep connected with real people.

There are hundreds of online screenwriting groups, too, that act as a forum for people to discuss screenwriting issues and developments, and that sometimes allow opportunities for people to share their work and receive feedback. There are two dangers with this kind of group, though. Firstly, the quality of such groups can vary enormously. Especially if you're trying to get useful feedback, you should be careful about who's using the groups and what's in it for them. If you never meet these people, it's often hard to get a real sense of what they know and what their agendas are. Second, it can be very easy to procrastinate when writing a screenplay – and constantly surfing the internet is potentially very dangerous. Because of the collapsing of space and time, using online groups can actually compromise the structure of your writing practice rather than enhance it. If, for example, you keep getting e-mails throughout the day – responding to a posting on an online forum – you could find yourself getting distracted, even hooked. On the other hand, if you're attending a regular 'real' writers' group, then you can plan your day around that one meeting, and physically take yourself out of the writing and into the group.

INDUSTRY INSIGHT

Christine Rogers is a Melbourne-based screenwriter and filmmaker. She's currently writing a low-budget genre feature, and developing two TV series, and has this to say:

On co-writing

Co-writing is the best of times and the worst of times, to paraphrase Dickens. I've co-written four long projects, one of which has been produced as a short feature. The co-writer of three of these (and the short feature) was also the director.

So, the best of times – let's begin there. Writing for me goes in fits and starts. Sometimes the work flows, other times I feel like my head's made out of wood. Sometimes I might have an idea and be so surprised and pleased with it that it goes straight away into the script – and it's only later, with time and reflection, that I understand suddenly that it won't work.

When I was co-writing, I would bring this new idea to our writing space and tell my co-writer and immediately she would take it and turn it over in her hands like a found object, and with that objectivity we could begin to look at all sides of it – all of its ramifications. So everything was tested, debated, discussed, before it got on the page. Ultimately, this made for much stronger work. And then there were those amazing moments when my co-writer would come up with an idea so absolutely different from anything that I'd ever think of. Together, the work we wrote was so much richer and more imaginative. We sat together at the computer and wrote and talked and talked and talked until I knew her just as well as any close friend. I don't know if you need to be that intimate to do good work, but we were. But, of course, with intimacy comes trust.

Now let's talk about the worst of times. You can call it creative tussle, or you can call it ego, but, if you're the co-writer writing with the director, ultimately they're going to have the final say. Unfortunately, I also direct, so this was sometimes a difficult experience for me.

There can be issues, too, if your heads aren't in the same film. There was a particular feature that sprang from one of the director's ideas. We talked it through and the idea was very sketchy. I went away and wrote the first draft, and when she read it she thought it quite different to what she had in her head – and she didn't particularly like it. But others liked it, and we were funded to write another draft. So we set about co-writing on it, but this was a disaster. She tried to push it back to the original idea she had in her head, and I – and the work itself – resisted. It never did find its place and has become an abandoned project.

Issues in my co-writing also arose because of input at different stages of development. I had a part-time job whereas my co-writer was able to write full-time, which meant she spent more time at the coalface. At first this was an irritation, but it soon turned to far worse.

As one project proceeded through multiple drafts, and got close to seeking production finance, the director began writing me out of the process – and the contract. The way it was going to work was that we'd split the (as usual, small) writing fee for the first few drafts, then after that she'd get the bulk of the money, and the copyright. I thought most of the hard work had been done in the first five or so drafts – two years' work – and she was now just making minor amendments (which I mostly didn't agree with). Her belief was that the later drafts were just as hard.

The producer sided with her – after all, she was the director. I felt hugely betrayed, as no doubt did she. The film never got made, but that's another story. After this experience, I vowed never to co-write again. However, five years later, I'm currently working on a fledging TV series with another writer, but she's not the director – nor am I – and the whole team-based TV thing works differently from the ego-driven world of the feature. I hope.

© Christine Rogers, 2012

WRITERS' EVENTS

Writers' events have already been mentioned as a valuable opportunity to meet people, keep up with industry developments, and pitch work. Whether these are festivals, conferences, workshops or talks – run by private organisations, industry bodies or writers' guilds – they can work as both an opportunity to develop and an opportunity to focus. In other words, you can use them to gain specific knowledge, contacts, or writing and funding opportunities, or you can use them as a focused target for your writing, such as having a pitch ready for this or a draft ready for that. In this way, you're not just turning up in the hope that you might meet someone or learn something – you're turning up with ideas and work that you've specifically prepared.

A good way of keeping up-to-date with writers' events is by joining organisations – such as writers' guilds and screen associations – and subscribing to newsletters. There are so many e-newsletters around these days that it can be hard to keep track of things, let alone read everything that's sent through. My advice here would be to subscribe only to the ones that you think you'll get something out of – such as local organisations – and to review your subscription lists every few months, to see if you can opt out of any. Sometimes you don't know how good or bad something's going to be until you try it. And another word of advice here – a lot of the daily or weekly e-newsletters you can subscribe to are actually nothing more than a way of advertising someone's book, workshop, consultancy service, etc. Of course, these are valuable ways of promoting such services, but I've seen too many that give very little to the reader and spend most of their time promoting how they can help them – for a fee. There's nothing wrong with these kinds of services – in fact I offer them myself – but there's a fine line between being genuine and being a charlatan. So read and choose wisely.

INDUSTRY INSIGHT

Mark Poole is an Australian filmmaker and screenwriter, and was also Chair of the Victorian Branch of the Australian Writers' Guild from 2007 to 2012. He has this to say:

What a writers' guild can do for you

As someone once said, it's not what the Writers' Guild can do for you, but rather what you can do for the Guild. Or is it? As a professional writer, you may feel that the Guild needs you more than you need it, but in my long association with the Australian

Writers' Guild (AWG), I firmly believe that, if you're serious about developing a screenwriting career, then the Guild is one way of establishing your bone fides.

Having been Chair of the Victorian Branch of the AWG for the past five years, and served as National Vice President for the five years before that, I'm obviously biased. But, looking back, I'm sure that the association has helped my career substantially. The Writers' Guild is a great way to meet and mingle with like-minded people who put writing first, and there wouldn't be many story producers, script editors or assessors on the Australian landscape who aren't also members. Not that it's a closed shop, but people who are interested in writing and understand the power of a great story naturally gravitate to the AWG.

So over the years I've benefitted in a host of practical ways through the friendships and networks I've built via the AWG. For example, it was a Guild stalwart who recommended my services to an Indian production company who wanted an Australian writer to research and write a documentary about India. And I'm sure he recommended me for the gig, not only because he knew I could accomplish it, but also in part because he knows how much time and effort I've put into the Guild. That's how the network works.

But there's another reason why a Writers' Guild is a powerful force for good for writers. It's an intangible one, about the sometimes elusive, even tribal sense of belonging that all writers need to cling on to, especially when the chips are down. Being a member is one way of reminding others, and yourself, of your status as a creator of works for performance, be it film, television, theatre, radio or online work.

Fifty years old in 2012, the Australian Writers' Guild was started to support performance writers, or those who pen the words and metaphors to be transformed into images or scenes on stage or screen. The AWG covers writers of film, television, theatre, radio and interactive media, and provides a welcome focus on the writing aspects of the craft, both in terms of centring the writer as a key driver in media where the director is more often regarded as the key, and in acknowledging the point that, even where a screenplay may never be written down (for example in some forms of documentary), some person or team has thought about the work from the point of view of the story, character and theme.

Other practical reasons why a Writers' Guild is powerful – in Australia it's the biggest by far of the main craft unions, having around 2,500 members, both full and associate. You can join without screen credits, but to be accepted as a full member you need to have written professionally, which means that membership is seen as proof you're the real deal.

One very practical offering of a Guild is the model contracts it can provide to ensure your work's provided with the most legal protection available. As well, a Guild employs legal staff who can steer you in the right direction, particularly at the early stages of a deal with a producer or production company. So if you're serious about screenwriting – serious enough to overcome the barriers, the criticisms and the barbs and carve out a viable writing career – there's no other way forward. A Writers' Guild offers access to a powerful network of screenwriters.

And what can you do for a Guild? The AWG began in the 1960s to campaign for better rates of pay for radio writers, a goal it managed to achieve, and in the 1970s the Guild negotiated better rates for television writers. Since then, the Guild has worked tirelessly on behalf of all performance writers to forge agreements with bodies such as the Screen Producers Association, television networks and theatre companies, and is in regular dialogue with government agencies such as Screen Australia.

Like most other Guilds, the AWG hosts regular events which put the writer centre stage, such as monthly meetings where invited guests talk about the art, craft and business of screenwriting. There's something refreshing, even heartening, to be in a roomful of writers who share your perspective on industry matters as well as your creative ambitions – even dreams.

© Mark Poole, 2012

Being part of the industry – which doesn't just mean working in it, but finding out about it – is also really important when considering future projects and working practices. For example, if you find out from an industry event that a production company is actively looking for children's films, you might want to think about reordering your future screenwriting plans to try and take advantage of this. Or, if you hear from a guest speaker that she's setting up a new funding scheme, and you know what the deadlines are going to be, you can work on your screenplay accordingly to try and take advantage of that.

Being a successful screenwriter is about being a storyteller and being connected. It's rare that a screenplay will sell on its own – usually, it needs its screenwriter to do the work and to meet the right people to get it somewhere. To be connected, you don't just have to know the right people – you have to know how to work with them. Creating strong relationships early on can do wonders for your career, not just because people might want to work with you again, but because people will join new networks and teams and introduce you to more people. Things can grow exponentially.

Joining forces with other people can also help to create new, innovative ideas – ideas that wouldn't have come from you alone. As well as clearly energising a project and giving it more momentum to go on and be made, working in such a team can help to push ideas more towards the original end of the spectrum. In turn, these innovations can be what make your work more successful and revered – awards, prizes, critical acclaim, etc. Thinking outside of the box – which a team approach can often do more effectively than an individual one – can also help to pave the way for the future of screenwriting and the industry. Everything had to start somewhere – the first crowd-funded film, the first web drama, etc – and so building a network, keeping connected and maintaining strong working relationships is one way of making sure that you're not left behind.

INDUSTRY INSIGHT

Award-winning producer Sue Maslin, whose credits include the features *Road to Nhill* (1997) and *Japanese Story* (2003) and the transmedia documentary project *Re-Enchantment* (2011), has this to say:

Some thoughts on the future of screenwriting

Once writers begin working in the non-linear, online environment, the first thing they need to let go of is the idea of directing audience engagement through narrative – there's no such thing as a beginning, middle and end. User attention span is measured in seconds (yes, seconds!) and so most of what screenwriters 'write' might never be seen. All script decisions have to be made in relation to user experience. The 'writer' is completely in the hands of the digital media director or developer (software programmer) as to what might or mightn't be realised within the digital parameters (software limitations, available memory, basic downloads, etc). This clearly has enormous implications for the content creator, that goes way beyond genre and budget.

Scripts in this environment are developed into maps – the navigational architecture of the site – and these, together with scoping documents, become the technical blueprint for online design. It's not uncommon for digital developers to never refer to a script in the way we've become accustomed to in film and television. On top of this, every element of the work needs to be broken down and managed via a Content Management System (CMS) – a database where the iterative process of design, programming and testing (and fix-ups involving further design, programming and testing) can be tracked by all members of the team at all stages of production.

I'm particularly interested in what happens to the creative process when the systems methodology requires you to work with a Content Management System – the flow of meaning, the possibility that 'the whole could be greater than the sum of its parts'.

Quite aside from User Generated Content (UGC), the idea of 'authorship' itself becomes problematic in an interactive environment, as users increasingly become 'authors' of their own experiences. The professional writer's vision – mediated by the developer as the site or application is built – is just part of the overall design experience delivered to users. Even the title 'writer' is becoming increasingly redundant, and often writers are brought in on a casual basis to deal with 'content' issues as they arise. Traditional notions of writer and director as 'author' have been largely replaced with titles such as 'experience designer'.

Some argue that digital developers are the new breed of content creators. The expression 'get with the program' all of a sudden takes on a deeper meaning if writers want a future in the online environment. It's a time of transition but there will always be a place for screen content writers of some sort – even if we're unsure what shape it'll take in the future.

© Sue Maslin, 2012

CONCLUSION AND RESOURCES

As I outlined in the Introduction, I set out to write a book full of ideas and inspiration, and useful for the screenwriter as a guide – not a manifesto – for creating wonderful screenplays.

The book has covered all aspects of the craft of screenwriting – from getting ideas and developing them, to structuring scenes and writing dialogue – as well as some of the more practical aspects of promoting and selling your work. The latter are often missing from screenwriting books, so it felt right to include them and combine them with the nuts and bolts of craft.

I learned a lot about screenwriting through writing this book. Really thinking deeply about how screenplays work has opened up new and fresh ideas for me to consider the next time I write and teach. For me, the case studies have provided a lot of this insight and inspiration. Whether learning about worlds through *Juno*, cast design through *The Kids Are All Right*, character voice through *Notes on a Scandal*, or theme through *Me and You and Everyone We Know*, analysing stories that work has crystallised even more my knowledge and understanding of how, as screenwriters, we write a story on the page that's intended for the screen. And I use the word 'through' quite deliberately here. We don't learn 'from' existing stories, because that's reactive and feels like we're trying to copy. Instead, we learn 'through' existing stories because we understand how things work and proactively apply them to our own practice.

RESOURCES

The following resources have been mentioned in the book, and are examples of what I think are good and useful references for any screenwriter. There are many, many more, of course, but these are the ones I personally have faith in.

Books

Aronson, L (2011), *The 21st-Century Screenplay: A Comprehensive Guide to Writing Tomorrow's Films*, Los Angeles: Silman-James Press

Ashton, P (2011), *The Calling Card Script: A Writer's Toolbox for Screen, Stage and Radio*, London: Methuen

Batty, C (2011), *Movies That Move Us: Screenwriting and the Power of the Protagonist's Journey*, Basingstoke: Palgrave Macmillan

Batty, C & Cain, S (2010) *Media Writing: A Practical Introduction*, Basingstoke: Palgrave Macmillan

Batty, C & Waldebäck, Z (2008), *Writing for the Screen: Creative and Critical Approaches*, Basingstoke: Palgrave Macmillan

Cain, S (2009), *Key Concepts in Public Relations*, Basingstoke: Palgrave Macmillan

Campbell, J (1993), *The Hero with a Thousand Faces*, London: Fontana Press

Dancyger, K & Rush, J (2006), *Alternative Scriptwriting: Successfully Breaking the Rules* (4th ed), Oxford: Focal Press

Davis, R (2008), *Writing Dialogue for Scripts* (3rd ed), London: A&C Black

Davis, R (2004), *Developing Characters for Script Writing* (3rd ed), London: A&C Black

Duncan, S (2008), *Genre Screenwriting: How to Write Popular Screenplays That Sell*, New York: Continuum

Field, S (2003), *The Definitive Guide to Screenwriting*, London: Ebury Press

Gulino, PJ (2004), *Screenwriting: The Sequence Approach*, New York: Continuum

Harper, G (ed) (2012), *Inside Creative Writing: Interviews with Contemporary Writers*, Basingstoke: Palgrave Macmillan

Hiltunen, A (2002), *Aristotle in Hollywood: The Anatomy of Successful Storytelling*, Bristol: Intellect

Hoxter, J (2011), *Write What You Don't Know: An Accessible Manual For Screenwriters*, New York: Continuum

Indick, W (2004), *Psychology for Screenwriters: Building Conflict in Your Script*, Studio City: Michael Wiese Productions

Jacey, H (2010) *The Woman in the Story: Writing Memorable Female Characters*, Studio City: Michael Wiese Productions

Kallas, C, (2010) *Creative Screenwriting: Understanding Emotional Structure*, Basingstoke: Palgrave Macmillan

Mahon, N (2011), *Basics Advertising 03: Ideation*, Worthing: AVA Publishing

McGilligan, P (1992, 1997, 1997, 2006, 2010), *Backstory* [series], Berkeley: University of California Press

McKee, R (1999) *Story: Substance, Structure, Style and the Principles of Screenwriting*, London: Methuen

Moritz, C (2008) *Scriptwriting for the Screen* (2nd ed.), London: Routledge

Owen, A (2004) *Story and Character: Interviews with British Screenwriters*, London: Bloomsbury

Rabiger, M (2005), *Developing Story Ideas: Finding the Ideas You Haven't Yet Had* (2nd ed), Oxford: Focal Press

Scott, KC (ed) (2005), *Screenwriters' Masterclass: Screenwriters Discuss their Greatest Films*, London: Faber and Faber

Seger, L (2011), *Writing Subtext: What Lies Beneath*, Studio City: Michael Wiese Productions

Seger, L (1998), *Creating Unforgettable Characters: A Practical Guide to Character Development in Films, TV Series, Advertisements, Novels and Short Stories*, New York: Henry Holt & Co

Vogler, C (2007), *The Writer's Journey: Mythic Structure for Writers*, Studio City: Michael Wiese Productions

Voytilla, S (1999), *Myth and the Movies: Discovering the Mythic Structure of 50 Unforgettable Films*, Studio City: Michael Wiese Productions

Waldebäck, Z & Batty, C (2012), *The Creative Screenwriter: Exercises to Expand Your Craft*, London: Methuen

Yoneda, KF (2011), *The Script-selling Game: A Hollywood Insider's Look at Getting Your Script Sold and Produced* (2nd ed), Studio City: Michael Wiese Productions

Magazines, journals and websites

Australian Short Films – www.australianshortfilms.com

The Australian Writers' Guild – www.awg.com.au

BBC Film Network – www.bbc.co.uk/filmnetwork

BBC Writersroom – www.bbc.co.uk/writersroom

The BFI – www.bfi.org.uk

British Council Film – www.film.britishcouncil.org

Celtx – www.celtx.com

Cinema16 (short films) – www.cinema16.org

Final Draft – www.finaldraft.com

Indiegogo – www.indiegogo.com

Inktip – www.inktip.com

Kickstarter – www.kickstarter.com

The London Screenwriters' Festival – www.londonscreenwritersfestival.com

MovieScope Magazine – www.moviescopemag.com

PleaseFundUs – www.pleasefund.us

Screen Australia – www.screenaustralia.gov.au

Screen International – www.screendaily.com

The Script Factory – www.scriptfactory.co.uk

Script Magazine – www.scriptmag.com

Shooting People – www.shootingpeople.org

Skillset – www.creativeskillset.org

The Smalls – www.thesmalls.com

Spanner Films (crowd funding) – www.spannerfilms.net/crowd_funding

Vimeo – www.vimeo.com

The Writers' Guild of America, East – www.wgaeast.org

The Writers' Guild of America, West – www.wga.org

The Writers' Guild of Canada – www.writersguildofcanada.com
The Writers' Guild of Great Britain – www.writersguild.org.uk
The Writers' Guild of New Zealand – www.nzwg.org.nz
YouTube – www.youtube.com

INDEX OF FILMS

creative ESSENTIALS

SHORT FILMS
...how to make and distribute them

ARTS REVIEWS
...and how to write them

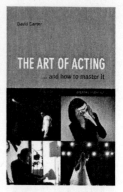

THE ART OF ACTING
...and how to master it

PLAYS
...and how to produce them

READING SCREENPLAYS
how to analyse and evaluate film scripts

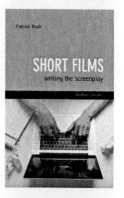

SHORT FILMS
writing the screenplay

DAN WILLIAMS
Web TV Series
how to make and market them...
creative ESSENTIALS

SCREENPLAYS
how to write and sell them

DOCUMENTARIES
...and how to make them

www.kamerabooks.com